Enlightened Beings:
The Awakening

SERRA COATE

Enlightened Beings: The Awakening

Copyright © Serra Coate 2023
First Edition

ISBN 978-1-914447-99-0

Prepared by TGH International Ltd.

www.TGHBooks.com

Love is the language of my soul as it dances gracefully through this life and interacts with all beings. Love is my guiding force. Love is my awakening. Love is all there is.

-Serra

Dedication

To my family, for your unwavering support and love as I follow my dreams and expand into all that I can be. I could not be here today without you.

To Source, for trusting me with these words and teachings. I am humbled, honored and in awe everyday with the gifts you continue to give.

To my spirit family on Earth, thank you for being my teachers, companions and steadfast sounding board as I navigate learning and expanding my knowledge and vibrational fields. What a fun adventure we are on!

To my Earth teachers and all the teachers that came before me, without your dedication to learning, following your dreams, Source, human enlightenment and vibrational expansion – I could not be here today. Thank you for paving the way.

To the Council of the Serraphine, who have repeatedly done this work with honor and sacrifice to prepare for this moment in time. For being my guiding light in the dark and the beacon on the horizon.

To the Children of the Future, the ones who will break the barriers, the ones who will propel this work, and propel the New Earth into the new vibrational stratosphere it is intended to be.

Contents

FOREWORD

We awaken the mind to the possibilities of this human life. We awaken every individual to the love that surrounds them, and by choosing love, they choose expansion. Expansion of the mind. Expansion of the soul. Expansion of their being and all they are capable of.

We are breaking the matrix of human life. We set free those souls that reach for more. Those souls that feel the greater world but do not know how to obtain it.

Reach for the stars and gain your starlight. The light that shines within you is more than your being. It is the cosmos shining through your eyes. The alignment of the stars is here to be your guide. It is to be your beacon. It is here to bring peace and joy to the planet and its people – a peace that is only known by finding yourself, finding your joy, and finding your purpose.

Allow the light within – that has been dormant for so many generations – to flood from your soul, and for your being to awaken the mind to your true potential. Your guiding light is love.

In love. Be love. You are love.

The light within you shines with the strength of many suns and is a force that created the world and gave life. Allow your light to bloom, to show your true potential and calling. The being within you is so much more than you will ever understand.

You are not a bystander in your life. You are the conductor.

–Channeled message from a Spirit Guide

Introduction

Believing in yourself and your dreams is the gateway to creating them.

The orange sunset intensifies along the horizon as the sun lowers in the sky. I rock gently on my porch swing enjoying the last of this beautiful October day. The sunset's vivid display is the result of a forest fire nearby, creating a hazy sky. I enjoy the beautiful display of color even though I am fully aware of the cause.

I reflect on my beautiful, blessed life with gratitude, while understanding that others are affected by the fires that are creating this smoke hovering in the sky. Others are touched by struggles and tragedy while I enjoy a leisurely swing. *How did I get so lucky?* Was it luck or was it learning the rules of the human experience and manifestation?

Two years ago, the world shut down due to COVID-19. My family faced many changes and yet those were happy years of togetherness and fun. We spent more time as a family and even vacationed most of the summer, camping at the lake and enjoying friends and family outside. I cherished these years – they gave me the perfect opportunity to spend precious time with my sons before they headed off to college and their own life adventures. What a beautiful gift of time and connection I was given.

I realize some of my happiest years were some of the most difficult for others in my community and even the world. How is there such great disparity in the human experience? I want everyone to live in love and joy, or at least have a choice in how they experience their human life.

Channeling this book gave me a new perspective on many things, especially natural occurrences (i.e. forest fires), life's challenges, and the suffering of people. Admittedly, my heart breaks for anyone who suffers. I wish everyone knew the principles of vibrational alignment to understand challenging and "unfortunate" events in a new way. We have the power to change our human experience; however, we are not taught how to use frequency, manifestation, or creation – the tools that help shift our experience. As a result, many wander aimlessly while doing the best they can with the limited information they have. An intention of this book is to equip you with the teachings and tools that will shift unfortunate events to fortunate ones. Struggle and hardship may still enter your life; however, it will be seen through a new lens of learning and embraced as an experience along the pathway to your highest vibrational self.

This channeled text presents information on how to understand the energetic world, how to choose your vibrational frequency, how to release energetic densities in your physical form, and how to make choices to align with the principles of the New Earth.

The world we know cannot survive in its current contrasting state and it is time to choose love, not fear. A time of human evolution and enlightenment is upon us. A time of change and a time of choosing love for ourselves, our neighbors, and our planet.

This book guides you in how to call forth your enlightenment, begin the awakening process, and reconnect your soul's light to Source. Start your journey to become all that you are and capable of being and more. Experience the freedom of uncapping your soul to expand into all of the possibilities within this human life, but also your soul within the cosmos. You are not small, so stop limiting who you are and who you will be. You can be free, limitless and an expanded version of you.

Authentic you. Soul-filled you. Limitless you.

To expand into the next version of you, you need to understand the human world you have created and understand the limitations and confinements you believe and have invested in. This is necessary to break free into the New Earth and its potential. To experience the New Earth, you will need to learn how to see the world around you differently – to see through a different lens with all the possibilities.

None of this is simple or easy. It takes choice and hard work. It takes time and perseverance. Yet, it leads to freedom (in every way) and a love for yourself and everyone around you. By calling forth the Awakening Process, you invite your soul to move into the driver's seat of your life – directing, guiding, and aligning with your inner desires, purpose, and universal understandings.

Set yourself free and walk into your awakening.

My awakening journey was atypical, yet we all have nudges, understandings, and breadcrumbs to follow. It is when we choose to follow the breadcrumbs that we find our path forward.

I was an unruly child who entangled myself in nature. Trees, bugs, serpents, and small creatures were my friends. I knew from a young age there was more to this human life than I could see with my eyes. I felt a call from the ocean inside my bones and a connection to the Earth when I walked barefoot on the ground.

As I grew older, I dismissed my 'knowingness' and attributed it to my family lineage of fisherman and my mother's hippy ways.

When I was 10 years old, I saw a ghost for the first time and my sense of reality shifted. I was sleeping over at a friend's house and watched an empty rocking chair move continuously for an extended period. At that time, it felt like the chair rocked for an hour, but in hindsight it was probably only 10 minutes. I felt alone and afraid. My friend had fallen asleep on the couch as we watched a movie, and I was paralyzed with fear. Everything about that moment is vivid in my mind, as though it happened only a couple years ago. I recall the room, the movie we were watching, and the rocking chair placement. At that moment, I knew I could not dismiss what I was witnessing. I knew I was watching a ghost. I knew it was a harmless grandmother watching over her family. And I knew there was more to this world than adults were telling me.

As I trembled in fear, I called on the angels to protect me... and they came. I remember the feeling of them comforting and protecting me. As I sensed their presence around me, I felt safe. From that moment forward, I would occasionally hear their comforting words that served as a guide throughout my life. I knew I could not tell anyone about the angels speaking to me, so I announced to friends and family that I saw a ghost. Most adults laughed and brushed off my comments and paid little attention to my experience of seeing a ghost. I did not mention that I could hear angels speaking to me out of concern that the adults would view this as hearing voices in my head. I didn't want them to think I had a mental illness or condition. I knew the feelings, knowingness, visions, and voices of my angels were there to help and protect me.

Why were angels speaking to me different then the self-propelled rocking chair? We learn at a young age what is acceptable in our society. We turn off our inner senses and our "connectedness" to the world around us because we are taught to. We learn what is "normal" and we innately conform to be accepted by our family, community, and society.

I wish I had known that my mother also heard angels and that they helped guide her throughout her life. My mother had a knowingness that there was more to this world than she could see with her eyes. She was a seeker. A seeker of connection and understanding. When I was 12 years old, my mother began participating in a meditation-based belief system called Sahaja Yoga Meditation. Through its teachings, I learned to work with my Kundalini Energy, understand the chakra system, and how to feel energy movement within my body.

Prior to Sahaja Yoga, my mother was our Sunday School teacher in our small-town church. My understanding of Jesus, God, and Angels were the soft fluffy kind; I knew them as only benevolent and kind. Inside my mother's heart, she knew God's love was gentle and kind. She continued to seek teachings that aligned with her inner knowing, and that is how she found Sahaja Yoga.

When I turned 30, a switch flipped inside of me and I had a phrase on repeat in my mind: *You are meant to do something, figure it out*. It was incessant, annoying, and only grew stronger as time passed.

For years, this phrase continued without much physical progress. I was a mother of three small children, and I did not have time to figure anything else out. I recall being exhausted, angry, and jealous that my husband got to leave and go to work every day, while I "did everything" at home. I was mad at life, and he was the target of my frustrations because I felt trapped. I remember standing at the kitchen sink one day washing dishes. I was irritated, tender, and my tears flowed without end. My angels came in with a message to focus on gratitude. *What are you grateful for today? What do you appreciate about your husband?* I took a deep breath, centered myself and started to shift my focus from anger to gratitude. I recognized the choice before me: I would either choose to continue with old patterns or choose happiness and change my thoughts.

For several months I thought of five things to be grateful for before I went to bed. When I woke up, I found five things to be grateful for. Every time I started to slip into anger or frustration, I found five things to be grateful for. As I continued to make gratitude my way of being, a shift happened within me. I did not understand it at the time, but I was raising my vibration with a very powerful emotion: Gratitude.

By focusing on gratitude, my life became happier. The struggles of my life were the same and life was still challenging at times; however, I saw my life differently. I saw that I had a roof over my head, food in my fridge and a husband who worked hard to provide for his family. I saw healthy children who were strong willed and would grow into strong-minded adults. I viewed my life through a different lens. My life did not change; however, my perception of my life had changed. What I chose to focus on changed, and as a result, my happiness grew.

The incessant mission of finding my purpose was still pushing its way forward. *You are meant to do something, figure it out.* While out to dinner with a friend, I mentioned this nagging mantra. "You should see my mother-in-law," she said. "She is a Reiki Master and could do a soul retrieval to help figure it out." My friend was speaking a foreign language. I did not know what Reiki, or a soul retrieval, was. We spent the rest of the dinner chatting about energy healing, past lives, Reiki, and Shamanism. I was excited with new concepts that made a lot of sense to me. I jumped into learning energy work and healing because it spoke to my soul in a way I couldn't describe. The 'knowingness' I had carried my entire life finally made sense! I had a tangible explanation for things that I knew but could never explain. I saw, felt, and understood the energetic world around me in new ways.

I entered a learning phase and took classes to become a Reiki Master. I studied 21st Century Shamanism, Energy Medicine, and later Light Language. I learned to connect with myself and the energetic world. I learned to 'journey' by going into a meditative state to enter the Spirit or Energetic World and learned how to safely navigate non-ordinary reality (everything around us we cannot see with our eyes). I gathered a team of protectors, teachers and allies, and learned to seamlessly communicate with them.

As my skills grew and my vibrational state increased, I had new opportunities open within the Energetic World. I was invited to work with the Council of the Enlightened. A member of the Council explained that the council focuses on helping humans become Enlightened Beings. I began to channel uplifting and inspiring messages from various council members. Initially, the process was exhausting and took great focus from my human brain. I had to concentrate on clearing my mind and focus on keeping my personal thoughts quiet, otherwise, I would lose the stream of dialog I was receiving. The best way I can describe the process of channeling is that I was in a meditative state of thoughtless awareness with a dialog flowing from my mouth. These were not my thoughts; these were words gifted to me. It took about a year of casually recording short messages to build my skills and proficiency.

I asked an Enlightened Being how he is able to speak through me:

"It is like standing in a rainforest with beams of light through the canopy leaves hitting the forest floor below. There are distinct rays of light, and energy is flowing. When you and I work together or you

speak with other Enlightened Beings, you are merely stepping into the ray of sunshine they are emitting to Earth.

You can move, walk away, and have control over your own physical thoughts. You are merely standing in a ray of light, energy, frequency, and connecting with that frequency, and we can transmit information to you. You interpret it and create the words.

Sometimes you stumble over your words and that is because you are interpreting the thought. I am not creating the words; you are using your own words. I am creating a thought process, a line of consciousness, and you are choosing the words that best represent what you are thinking. "

When I enter the Spirit World, it feels like so much more than stepping into a ray of light. For me it feels like I am stepping into a movie set with vivid colors, complete with unique beings, visceral emotions, and physical sensations. Our human bodies were meant to connect with the spirit world in this way; doing so allows our minds to come alive and expand. It is so much more than just imagination. It is more than a vivid dream – in the spirit world, you can touch, feel, and think with limitless possibilities. It is so much more than I can even explain.

Unexpectedly, God appeared in a journey and asked me to channel a text for the New Earth and to teach people how to ascend to the New Earth. He said the text would be a road map to enlightenment. I felt honored, humbled, and a deep sense of responsibility to accurately represent the messages flowing through me.

I began channeling messages with God in September 2018. The process was slow and methodical. Looking back, I see a different view of the experience than what I understood at the time. As I channeled more teachings, I had to vibrationally align with the information presented to me. I had to understand the significance, have the vocabulary, and understand the concepts flowing through me.

I diligently channeled messages, sometimes only once every couple of weeks. I'd lock myself away in my guest/meditation room and settle into a nest position in the bed. I'd put in my ear plugs, cover my eyes with my eye mask, and use my phone voice recorder to capture the information that would come through. I entered a deep meditation to hold God's flow of consciousness.

I worked with many teachers in the Spirit World, and they always knew the plan for my journey. Sometimes, I requested to visit God to channel a new teaching but would instead be brought on another adventure to learn, ask questions, or understand new concepts. I had to increase my knowledge and understanding before I was ready to bring forward the next teaching.

On days that I would meet with God, my Spirit Teacher would bring me to what I named, "God's House," with an intricate spiral staircase leading to an ordinary looking door. Sometimes, I would knock and other times I would excitedly burst through the door. I know everyone who visits God's House has a different experience with what it looks like, and occasionally it changes depending on what we are doing. Inside the house is a cloud-like room with wispy white floors, walls, and ceilings. The room is expansive yet feels purposeful and comfortable. There is a large sitting area with two white couches facing each other and a white coffee table between them. The couches grow or shrink depending on the number of people they need to accommodate. Behind the couch is a small round bistro table where I often sit to channel messages. Typically, there are three chairs present – sometimes, there are two to four.

When I began to channel messages, my Spiritual Teacher, was always with me and the three of us (God, my Spiritual Teacher, and myself) would hold hands to start the channeling session. As I've grown, only God and I hold hands. I purposefully allow my mind to surrender into a 'thoughtless awareness state,' allowing God's thoughts to flow through my mind. Sometimes the thoughts are accompanied by pictures, diagrams, or other visuals to help understand the information. At times, I can feel God sifting through my vocabulary, choosing multiple words, feeling my association to a word, or saying many words to fully encompass the concept or idea.

Thoughts and words would flow from my mind and mouth easily and effortlessly, as long as I remained in a deep state of meditation. I had to practice grounding my physical and energetic bodies to be successful. In the beginning, I would sometimes start to 'drift' away and would be reminded to ground my physical and energetic bodies to hold the connection.

When I began channeling messages in 2018, I had already been journeying (connecting with guides in the Spirit World) for four years; however, this was a next-level skill. I had to focus, surrender, and be willing to allow God to flow through me. There is a freedom with a deep connection like this. All of God's words have deep emotion and love attached to them. I could feel the deep love and compassion he feels for all humans. He loves every being in existence with unconditional love.

The enormity of his love cannot be expressed in words. (I wish the English language had more words to describe love.) His embrace feels like being wrapped in a warm blanket of safety, protection, total acceptance of who you are, support in every desire you have, and immense gratitude for who you are at your core. There is never judgment; there is only choice and experience, only gratitude for choosing him and his teachings. My heart and mind feel like there are infinite possibilities of what I can do, be, and understand. He is our biggest cheerleader, teacher, and guide, but we must do the vibrational work to be ready for and to fully understand his teachings. He is willingly tethered by energetic laws to respect our free will. He can only teach me a topic after I have created the desire for the knowledge, which can make learning tricky.

The first time I visited God's House, I met the Seraphim Angels, and we had a lovely reunion. They were kind, funny, welcoming, and embraced my presence. God explained the frequency of love and how the Seraphim contain a rainbow of frequencies that together is the full spectrum and frequency of love. We are at a time of change and many humans today have come with a special job to bring in the frequencies of love to Earth. God showed me how to think about vibration and frequency in new ways using the rainbow, angels, and the human experience to lay the foundation of what was to come.

God's teachings are still coming through in 2022. In these four years, I have channeled teachings, deepened my understanding of frequency, of the ascension process, the New Earth, and my life purpose. My enlightenment journey is unfolding so I can teach others and show them the way to the New Earth. My desire to understand, ascend, and teach allows God to bring forth the information I share with you.

I use the term "God" in these messages because of my early Christian upbringing. I identify the consciousness of the universe as God because that is what my unconscious mind identifies Source as. He has no label except for the ones I create in my mind. He is not a *he*, even if that is how I identify him. I chose to use "him": however, you can identify 'The Consciousness of the Universe' in whichever way you choose. As you read through this book, I encourage you to use the name or concept that you are most comfortable with. As a consciousness, he is all and none of these, so we are all correct. He understands our human need to categorize and label, and he has no attachment to the way I see him. He will present to a person in a way that makes them feel most comfortable. Possibly, he will speak through the trees, or visit in a dream, or present as a mouse. As you read these messages, I ask that you remove all your preconceived notions of who God is and let yourself form new perceptions. I ask that you understand it is never about him, it is only about you.

Part 1

THE HUMAN CONDITION

CHAPTER 1:
THE BEGINNING

That which you are, you have always been.

THE BEGINNING

*I descend into a deep meditation and emerge in spirit form. I enter a wispy, ill-defined room with a small round bistro table with three chairs. God enters, warmly greets me, then says:

Hello, my sweet child. You have come to start our work. Let us begin with a blessing:

Oh, sweet Benevolent Ones, the ones who have come for so many years, the ones who do the work, the ones who bring the faith, the ones who pour the dreams, I welcome you here.
I welcome the Ancestors who have walked upon the Earth for many years.
I welcome the Descendants, the ones who will walk the Earth.
The Intergalactics who provide so much support.
The worldly leaders.

The work we do here is pure.
It has the best intentions for all of humanity.
Hold faith, hold true, and watch the beyond.
There is so much more to come, so much light, so much joy, and so much peace!

The best of everyone.

Let me tell you a story about a young woman who lived in a small village.
She loved her people, so she did everything she could for their betterment.
There was darkness along the horizon; a kind of darkness that her world had never seen before.
She lived in peace.
She lived in harmony.
The darkness was a type of evil that crept into people's souls.
It made good people become dark.

The only way to not be consumed by the darkness, was to fight. Not a literal fight – it was not violent – but the fight within one's head. Or you could say, they had to choose the light. They had to watch everything die and decay around them: Friends, family, trees, and living beings.

They had to choose happiness.
They had to choose forgiveness.
They had to choose to be kind.

There is a fight inside every human that darkness has touched, and that is what is going on today.
There is much going on around every one of you.
You can see darkness.
You can see cruelty, or you can see light.
You can see happiness.
You can see kindness.
This choice is what divides the New Earth from the Old.
The Old will be consumed in darkness, in pain, in hatred, in hurt, and those who choose to see those things, to dwell on those things, will go with it.

Those who see the light, feel the light, choose the light – the light of forgiveness, the light of beauty, of joy, of love – will move to the New Earth. You will join a group of like-minded who also see the light, choose the light, and choose the joy. You will create a new world. This will be difficult for many. This will be simple for others.

We are in a grand time: A time of change, a time of growth, and a time of joy.

The human experience has many choices, facets, prisms, which is why souls come to Earth.

You are multidimensional and you must learn how to use and harness your power.
There are limitless possibilities.
You are energy.
I am energy.
The Earth is energy.

A thought in your mind is energy, and you must learn to work with energy. Learn to master your energy. You will create a new world with this energy. Feel this energy.
There is immense beauty, there is immense love all around you.
Feel this love; feel this joy.
This is where you must stay.
This is what will carry you on.

No one is testing you, except for yourself.
Release. Let go.
Change thought patterns.
Change behaviors.
Change yourself.
To become who you choose to be.

You have a choice, you all have choices, but it starts with your thoughts.

No one can do this for you, it must be done by you.

Be okay with those you leave behind.

If they choose something different, you cannot save them.

They must do it themselves.

Love, that is what I am asking: Love.

*I sought further clarification on the above channeled message. Below is the message I received.

Serra: God, who was the woman you were talking about?

God: Why, it is you, my child. You chose to come here right now. You chose this work. You are a missing link that we needed to bring this message at this time. You have been preparing your whole life for this.

You chose to be humble.

You chose family.

You chose before you ever came to Earth what this life will be.

You chose your children.

You chose your spouse.

You chose your parents.

You chose each of them, what they bring to you, and what you needed to learn.

You came together.

You are where you are supposed to be, doing what you are supposed to be doing.

You have made it, but there is so much more to come, and so much more to DO!

Embrace this, be okay with this.

Your path – and everything you do – has been laid out with the best intentions for all humanity. Some of it will be hard. Some of it will be difficult, and we appreciate you and your sacrifices.

Know that we are here for you, and you are protected. Stay in the New Earth, bring the joy, bring the rays of light. People are seeking, and you are a beacon to show them the way. You have so much to bring.

Go my child and be with your family. The work has started, and you have started. Feel the joy in you, let it surround you, and your house, with everyone in it, radiate the joy, because you are there.

THE POWER OF LIFE IS FOUND WITHIN

The power of life is found within.
That power is within your soul; it is a glowing ember traveling through time, space, and matter.
It is a consciousness that lives within every being. Every being that is alive, dead, dying, yet to be born, a whisper, a raindrop, or thought; it is all encompassing.
There is life around you everywhere you look.
This life takes many forms.
Many consciousnesses.
See the world around you as energy.
As life.
As thought.

What is thought?

Thought is an electric pulse through your brain.
Thought triggers an avalanche of hormones.
Thought triggers a memory, a vision, an emotion, love, joy, peace, humbleness.

These thoughts shape your internal environment.
These thoughts not only change your body, but they also change

your energy, your cells, your mitochondria, and your DNA.

These thoughts change your energetic field.
Vibrations roll off you into the space immediately around you.
The vibrations do not stop there, they continue to roll and make their way around the planet. You can change the vibration of this entire planet. As you continue to raise your vibration level – with happiness, with joy, with peace, with tranquility, and with love – it affects those around you. Your vibration touches each and every person who walks into the room or comes into an elevator with you.

Your energetic field changes your family.
It changes how you interact with your spouse or children.
It influences how your child grows in the womb.
Know that your thoughts create your being.

You are social creatures.
Humans were meant to live together.
You were meant to be in harmony, in community, and in service.
It is programmed into your DNA.
These programs do not only affect you.

You also have a collective consciousness: A shared energetic field with all humans.
You affect each other.
This collective consciousness is splitting and dividing into two.
The higher vibrational frequencies such as love, happiness, and joy are separating from the denser vibrational frequencies of fear, anger, and despair.
What will you choose your vibrational frequency to be?

As the human collective consciousness divides, everything will appear the same.
Everything will appear chaotic and busy in the world.

However, there are vibrational pockets of joy, of peace found within – within yourself, within your mind, within your family, within your friends, within your household, and within your community.

Where do you find your joy?
Stay there. Live there. Be there.

Live in this joy because joy is the answer. Acceptance and unconditional love are the answer.
The more you love yourself, the more you accept yourself, and the more you give yourself unconditional love, the more you have to share. There is an infinite source within you.
Find your peace. Find your joy. Find your Love.

CHAPTER 2:
THE THREE BROTHERS

The greatest accomplishment of your life will be to follow your dreams.

THE THREE BROTHERS

I invited you here today to tell you a story. A story of an old wise man who wished to give his sons gifts.

The first son was wise. He was book smart and could figure everything out. The old man gave this son the gift of compassion. His middle son was scared. He saw life as a dangerous place, so he gave this son security.
His youngest son was playful and kind, but had no real focus, so he gave this son purpose.

The gifts the old man bestowed upon his three sons were placed inside their hearts.
The wise man helped the gifts grow, and when his sons were ready, their gifts would bloom. The sons had to choose to receive these gifts, even though they were already inside their hearts. They did not need to use them.
It was their free will.

The first son chose not to use his gift. He grew up to be a wealthy man; however, without compassion in his heart, he was mean. He was alone even when his family was around him. He could not feel their warmth, and he lived a lonely life.

The middle son was afraid to go out, so he did very little and stayed secluded. This son chose to consider his gift. He rolled it around in his mind and he thought about how the gift of security would work with his life. At one point, he allowed this gift to move into his heart and bloom. As a result, he saw the world as a different place. Life was safe and fun. In his adult years, he enjoyed everything immensely. He traveled, explored the world, and was well-read. He lived a happy life.

The third son was always playful, kind, and thoughtful. This son also chose to accept his gift. When he opened his gift of purpose, it led him to new places as he developed his gift into who he was as a person.

One day while enjoying nature, a golden door opened in front of the third son. He had a choice: To stay upon the land that was familiar, or to open the mysterious door and experience a new life.

The third son opened the door.
As he walked through, he saw a magical landscape of flowing rivers, steep mountains, snowy white peaks, and gorgeous waterfalls. It looked similar to the land he knew, however, there was something magical about this place. It was pristine and he could feel harmony and love on the wind. It was the vibration of the land, of the trees, of the flowers, and the birds. The vibration came upon the wind and wrapped everything in love.

He wanted to know more.
He wanted to feel more.
Everything felt possible there.
He felt light, without a care in the world. Worries just drifted away.

He explored the forest and greeted the small creatures, who seemed to understand him. This was so different from the world he left behind. He went to the river below and looked at his reflection. He saw bright glowing hair, freckles upon his nose, long fingers and toes, and a glow within him – a glow of happiness he had never seen before. It was as if every care he ever had disappeared.

There were no cares.

There was no worry.

There was only love.

There was only compassion.

There was only benevolence, kindness, infinite joy, infinite happiness, and laughter.

It began to rain. It was a warm rain that splashed upon his face, and he smiled. He put his hands out and looked at the water droplets in his palm. They glowed with a golden, shimmering light. The sun shined down on him and felt inviting. It enveloped him in a blanket of happiness and warmth.

What is this place? How can this be?

He thought of his family and brothers, and said, "I need to bring them here. This is the most magical place I have ever seen."

He walked back to the door he had entered from the forest. When he arrived, he thought, "Do I want to leave this place? Will I ever be able to come back?"

He decided he wanted to live in this magical land long term, but he needed to share it with the world.

He needed everyone to know about this new land and what was possible.

He opened the door and walked back into the darkness of the old world.

He felt a cold chill.

He felt a heaviness.

He felt despair and thought, I want to go back, but I need to share this with the world.

He found the middle brother, and said, "There is a magical place I want to show you! Will you come with me?" At first, his brother was afraid. He had opened his gift of security and safety but did not incorporate it into his heart. After further consideration, he felt he was up for the adventure.

The middle brother followed his brother to the door. When they arrived, the younger brother said, "Look! There it is." The middle brother said, "I don't see anything. I only see a rock wall."

The younger brother was confused. He thought, *how is this possible? How can I see the door and you cannot?* The younger brother opened the door and looked inside at the bright shimmering waters of the river below. The middle brother still only saw a rock wall. The younger brother left the door open and sat down to think, the middle brother sat down with him.

The younger brother asked his older brother to think about the most wonderful place he could imagine. The younger brother began to describe the land that he saw, how it felt, and asked his brother to picture these wonderful things. He described the happiness, the rays of sun upon his face, the warmth, and the joy he felt.

The middle brother closed his eyes and felt his heart open. He felt a warm sensation of happiness, gratitude, and unconditional love erupt inside him. He thought of everything that made him happy. He concentrated hard with his eyes closed and face scrunched.

When the middle brother opened his eyes, he saw the door. He saw that it was open and what lay on the other side. The two brothers walked through the door together. They ran and played like they were children again. They spent the entire day having fun and enjoying themselves.

Being one with nature.

Being one with each other.

Being one with the Earth, in happiness and with love.

As nighttime came, the brothers decided they needed to go back and share this with their families.

They went back to their third brother, the oldest, who was analytical and science based. The brothers described the beautiful place they both experienced. The older brother was curious, but skeptical. The following day, they brought their oldest brother to the door.

The oldest brother did not see the door, while the middle and younger brothers saw the door immediately. They asked their older brother to concentrate and think about the happiest thoughts he could imagine.

It took a while, maybe even weeks or months.

It took concentration.

It took acceptance.

It took forgiveness.

It took layers upon layers of shedding his learned ways.

He eventually found the gift of compassion buried deep inside his heart that had never been opened. He focused on it and allowed compassion to flow through him, with acceptance and release. He began to see the outline of the door.

The older son saw what was possible, however, he was not there yet to see the full door. So, he worked hard to increase his vibration by increasing his ability to love, and his depth of love. Over time he shed the layers that were conditioned by the current world and released them. He released and continued to let go of the conditioning, and eventually walked through the door with his brothers.

The three brothers and their families lived in harmony, in peace, in joy, and in high frequency together. They taught many more how to see the door.
They showed them the way.
They showed them how to release.
How to grow, and how to ascend.

Ascension is within you.
You only have to be willing to do the work to get there.
The work is within yourself – no one can do the work for you.
It is about releasing old ways, thought patterns, and healing old wounds.
And Forgiveness.

The only way to see the door is through vibrational alignment.
As one becomes happier, finds joy, lives in gratitude, and raises their vibrational level, they move forward. This is how you move forward.
How you ascend.
How you release is through forgiveness and kindness.

Ultimate joy is available to you.
Ultimate joy is available to all of you. It is a choice within every person.
Some need to be shown the way to find their golden door.

Find your inner light.

Grow this light, grow this joy, and you, too, will ascend.

CHAPTER 3:
THE TIPPING POINT

Allow the thoughts of your past,
to teach you what you no longer want.

THE BURDEN

Today, there is a lesson of the burden. The burden is a teaching, a progress, and is humanness. This humanness started many generations ago when the disconnect between the Spirit World and humans began. Humans were once part of the natural flow and walked between the lines of spirit and ordinary reality. This ebb and flow allowed them to transfer information, to readjust and evolve. Part of this evolution was developing oneself and developing the human collective consciousness.

The pathway for humans to become Enlightened Beings has been developing over thousands of years. Humans grew and changed, and within that, changed the structure of the human consciousness and human understanding.

There have been many teachers that have come to Earth with different purposes and lessons to be learned. We are now at the final tipping point. Humanity can teeter totter for only so long, sliding one way or the other.

The human collective consciousness needs to evolve and for that to happen, those seeking enlightenment must wake up and realize what humanity is. They must realize what this human life is and reconnect to the Spirit World.

When I say spirit, I do not mean those who have passed or who are deceased, or the realm of God or Angels. Those are all parts of the Spirit World, but I mean this in a greater sense. **Understanding that everything has a spirit**: The trees, the rocks, the ocean, every living being, each blade of grass, and recognizing the human role on this planet.

Humans have become disconnected to the planet and overrun with Ego.

What do we do now? We are at the tipping point.

I can tell you what is going to happen: The human collective consciousness will break and there will be two ways to go. There will be a ripping and a divide. That is what is to come. That is what your lifetime will hold, as well as the lifetime of your children and your grandchildren.

However, there is light!
There is so much light!
So much beauty!

When one chooses to live within that light, the divide will be a graceful journey.
Those who choose to stay in the dark – the unaware, the egoic – will have a very different experience.
The wonderful experience of Earth is that you have free will.
Many people have chosen darkness on an unconscious level, which has created the reality of this planet; however, many are choosing the light.

Within the principles of the universe, we cannot continue to live with these two polar energies or vibrations competing with each other. Thus now, they are dividing.

What is truly happening is there are two different realities on Earth that are divided by a vibrational plane. There is a gray layer between the Light and Dark and most people bob up and down, passing in between the light and the dark. Some people are a bit higher in the gray plane, where some are a bit lower.

Currently, this planet does not educate people about vibrations. If you look, if you seek, then you will see that it is right there. The teachings are right there!

It is vibrational quality.
You cannot live with one vibrational intention, thought process and creation, and then have your physical actions to do something different. You must decide and these must meld.

How does one rise their vibration? Choice, thought, and love.
Humans are beings of love.
Live in love for everyone and everything.
Love, and be grateful.

Love, and be kind.
Love, and embrace those who are different, and those you do not understand.
And love yourself.

Love everyone around you.
Live within this love.
Live within this grace.
Release anything that is not love.
Tell yourself, you are love.
You give love.
You spread love.
That is all there is in the upper vibrational world: Love.

To get to the New Earth you need to live in love every chance you get. Every opportunity is a chance for you to live in love. And it will become easier.

The more you love, give love, and receive love, the more it comes back to you.

The more everything falls into place.

The easier it gets.

Everything else falls away.

Allow it to fall away.

Allow it to become easy, because you have ultimate free will.

You can choose to bring it back.

You can choose to drop down lower in vibration and that is okay.

However, if your goal is to rise into the New Earth, then choose the frequency of love.

You do that by being in love, by giving love, and staying in a place of gratitude.

These are very powerful vibrations.

Understand, this is a choice.

It is a choice, and you are loved no matter what you choose.

REMEMBERING

I am carrying a large rose quartz angel statue that I place in the middle of the table.

Serraphine, thank you for bringing this wonderful gift. This will help pass the knowledge of the Akashic Records – the knowledge of the Universe, of an infinite life, of the Eternal Beings – into human consciousness.

Existence is so much more than life on Earth.
Your human life is only a grain of sand within a sandy beach that goes on for miles and miles.

The Akashic Record – all knowledge, of all times, and of all beings – is stored within this crystal. Quartz crystal is an amazing transfer of information. It absorbs vibrations, knowledge, and wisdom that we wish to transport into the human consciousness.

For humans to evolve, this information must be remembered.
The remembering process will be difficult for some.
The remembering process will release much of the Human Condition.
Remembering will bring the human consciousness back to the elemental phase.
The elemental phase is understanding that we are energy and we are light.

The frequency you emit is your light.
Some of you are beacons on Earth, to be guides, to show others, and lead the way.
All spirits who came to Earth, came with a humble purpose.
Everyone came with a purpose, even if that is to experience humanness, to experience pain, or to experience suffering.
In the Spirit World, suffering is a foreign concept.
Unfortunately, somewhere along the way, things got a little lopsided on Earth.

How do we correct the ship and right things to get humanity pointing in the direction of Light?
It is a choice and your free will that chooses the new direction.
Part of this transition is Remembering.

What are you Remembering?
At the core, you must remember that you are Spirit.

Remember that you are so much more than a physical body.
Remember the many lives you lived before.
Remember your purpose for being on Earth.

Why did you come?

Why do you choose to be on Earth now?
Those choices help shape your human experience, but the human experience is only part of the story. **The Soul that resides within all is an eternal being, an eternal life force. When released from the human body and the human consciousness, the soul is infinite love.**
Love is the vibration at the core of all things.

The purpose of this crystal today is to pulse the vibration of love; to pulse the vibration of the New Earth – of this eternal and wonderful experience for humans.

EGO & HUMAN COLLECTIVE CONSCIOUSNESS

For today's meeting I am wearing a necklace that would only be seen on a queen. It features large, emerald cut diamonds that circle my neck and a walnut sized, tear-drop shaped stone suspended from the center.

Come, come my child. Come sit, there is much to discuss. I asked you to bring a diamond tonight – a diamond of status, a diamond of wealth, a diamond of immense monetary value. Yet, I feel you shying away from this symbol of wealth. Why?

"I don't want to feel like I'm showing off and it alienates people."

This is still human Ego.
Human ego is that which places value on these inanimate objects.

In your case, it may be benign because you understand that which your culture has put value.

You will find in the New Earth there is not value in this way.
We still enjoy things and beautiful objects, but they are accessible to all.
Let this be a symbol of the New Earth that is inclusive, accepting, and freely given to those around you. There is value in beauty, there is value in the feeling it evokes within you, but there is no value in judgment.

Enjoy what is around you.
Enjoy the luxuries of this human life and the comforts you are given.
Enjoy the opportunities that you have been given, but also freely give, freely allow, because when you give you create a circle.
When you give, it will return. Have faith that it will return.

The more you give freely, the more it may return freely to you.

Possession also has an egoic factor; it is not quite ego, but a facet.
If you allow things to flow around you – possessions, people, love – know it will freely be returned.

Help those around you.
Help guide them to understand this concept. Help them understand that energy is free-flowing – it's always surrounding and embracing them.
Look at it as a free-flowing of your energy – your divine vibration – and give that freely to others.
The more you share energy, happiness, understanding, intelligence, consciousness, intuition, understanding, thoughts, the more that is accessible to others.

Embrace this giving.
Embrace this flow because it opens the door for it to return.

Let there be happiness.
Let there be support.
Let there be kindness in an infinite way.
Let it infinitely surround you and it will have a rippling effect around the planet.
Your vibrations affect those closest to you, and their vibrations affect those who are close to them. This spreads infinitely around the planet.
We are all connected.
We are all energy.

You are not only connected through vibration and energy in the physical plane; you are also connected in the vibration and frequencies of your thoughts.

This is the human collective consciousness.
This collective consciousness is connected to every living person and gives information to your unconscious mind. Humans do not have the tools to understand it yet, but that does not mean it is not real.

Energetically downloaded information will be used by others to spread the love of the New Earth, the frequency of the New Earth, and the technologies of the New Earth and by those who are developing technologies to prove Quantum Mechanics, the Infinite Light, and Akashic Record.

You are at the precipice of humanity's evolution.
There is much that will be changed, not only in your physical surroundings, but also the technology of the planet.   The technology of being able to transmit thoughts to one another.

This is what will come next.

You will support this technology and the development of it within the human consciousness. There are other worlds, other planets with other beings, Enlightened Beings, who are here to help you. We call them Intergalactics and they have been gracious to help share their technologies, because this will elevate the human race.

Humans will be able to work in sync with these other beings, with these other intelligences, but to do that there must be developments. There must be knowledge that is exchanged between the two entities, and this will happen through information that will be downloaded through you into human consciousness.

Human Consciousness is more than a memory bank.

It is a network.

It is an internet between all humans, and truly all living beings. There are other beings that access your unconscious mind.

A new technology will be downloaded into the human consciousness that will be used by others around the planet. Some in Australia, England, The Netherlands, Canada, and South America are developing these energy technologies simultaneously.

Once the information is put into the human consciousness, it will transmit through thought waves, energy patterns and frequencies that flow around every person.

It will allow the people seeking the spark of thought, intuition, and new ideas to pull details of the newly downloaded technology from the collective consciousness.

This technology will be developed simultaneously in three different locations around the planet.

The same technology, the same thought, in three different people's minds.

These people are not connected and are unknown to each other and have no idea this technology and thought process is being worked on by anyone else.

It will be created for all and will elevate the human race.

It will elevate those who wish to join in the New Earth – in love, in joy, and in endless possibility.

It will be used on an infinite scale.

It will allow thoughts between Intergalactics to speak freely between humans.

This will be a learned skill.

Seek this information in the future.

Seek the knowledge that is to come.

You will know what you need to learn by how it makes you feel.

Feel it deep inside. Feel it inside your deepest levels of thought, of consciousness, of enlightenment and you will know which one it is.

HUMANITY

Let's define humanity.

Humanity is not only that which is human, but all aspects of being human.

The mind that you have.

The limbs that you carry.

This humanness is the life you live, your interaction with others, and your fascinating existence together.

This is humanness.

To be honest, you haven't quite figured it out – although some cultures have more than others.

There is a need for humans to live collaboratively.

To live in communion with each other.

To live collectively within one organization or organism.

This will also develop in time, where each person flows in and out of this organism of humanity – a colony, a collective, a community.

Each person provides an essential service.
All are honored, appreciated, and important.

The life that you lead now is one of happiness, family, and seclusion.
The life that you are going into is one of joy, bliss, and community.

The community that you were intended to live in.
Community is programmed into your DNA.
Community is a concept that has been missing from most people, and it has greatly affected their mental health.
Community is the support and love from one another, and I truly mean unconditional love. Unconditional love is what you were intended to vibrate to support each other.

Within the community exists a need to understand give and take, ebb and flow, a giving and receiving – this is how humans were designed.
This ebb and flow are how humans survived thousands, even millions of years.
You will create a new tribe, which you have already started.

Your community will grow larger, and it will get more complicated, until everyone gets the hang of it.
Why do you need your community?
Why do you need to support one another?
Everyone cannot be everything, and that is the beauty of community.
Everyone gets the chance to rise above and shine with their strengths.
Everyone brings something different to the table, and that is a beautiful thing.

So, embrace people's differences and strengths, and see them as that.

This is an important part of living in a community and being harmonious.

It is not always easy, but with the understanding that everyone is loved, everyone is appreciated, and everyone has a role to play in creating a harmonious community.

Walk forward with a selfless mind set.

It will bring harmony and peace, and the understanding of community that is missing.

It will fill your hearts with joy and love.

DREAM WORLD

Today is about the Dream World.

The Dream World is not quite reality, not quite your unconscious mind, and not really a place at all.

The dream world is a mix, a hybrid.

We attempt to give you messages.

We show you your fears.

We also show you many ways to adjust.

Unfortunately, many humans have lost the ability to dream, to remember their dreams, or see vividly in their dreams. This has to do with their connection to the spirit realms.

When you go to bed at night, think about things that make you happy and things that you enjoy. Do not focus on what you need to do, build, or discuss, but rather happiness. This will open the door to enlightenment and will also put you in a higher vibration as you sleep.

This higher vibration will help resonate and build your vibrational levels.

The point of being human is to be happy.

We will show you ways to improve your happiness, have fun, and dream.

There are many things going on in the world today.
Many things are here to teach you, help you, and guide you.
You are to find these teachings and explore them.
You are to look at them from all angles.

The spirit world does not give answers in a linear way.
It is not how we think because we are not a linear world.
We see past, present, and future, and understand the importance of free will.

The interpretation of the information is part of the answer.
You may hear the exact same words in a year or two, and have a completely different answer, solution, or response.
The words that I tell you may be said the same to someone else,
but they will mean something different to someone else.
The same words to two different people can mean and feel very different.

Understand that we are working in many planes.
There is the Earth.
There are solar systems, galaxies, and intergalactic beings.
There are atoms, particles, and quantum mechanics,
and all of these are intertwined on an energetic level.
So, the energy put into words, feelings and thoughts travel throughout all these planes. They twist and turn, then come back around.
They do not dissipate the way that some think of energy.

When you get to a place in your life you are unsure of, feel the trees, the leaves, the wildlife, the birds, the soil, and the layers of Earth beneath you.
Feel the native peoples who have walked before you, learn and

understand their ways. You have had many teachers, and teachers come in all different forms.
Love and connect.

There is so much more that you cannot see, but you can feel.
Reach out with your heart.
Reach out with your mind.
Reach out with your emotions.
Reach out to connect to all living beings.
Feel the connection deep inside you.
Let them share their energy and their feelings.
Love and connect.

There is so much wisdom around you all the time.
You only need to look and ask.
Feel the connection to the Earth deep within, let it wrap around your belly and insides.
Let it heal you.

There are many more ways to heal than what you currently have. Medicine has not connected the energetic, emotional, and spiritual reasons for ailments.
Sometimes, people take on the energies of their physical world and transfer it into themselves.

Make sure to connect with the ground, let your feet dig into the soil and release.
Release any worries.
Release any cares.
Feel the energy moving through the Earth,
through the bottom of your feet,
and allow the cleansing energies of the Earth to pull the impurities in your life from you.
Do this while standing on soil, grass, or sand.

If you do not have these readily available, till a place in your garden, backyard, side yard, preferably where you feel comfortable. This may be hard to do in some winter months so instead, visualize yourself digging your toes in the soil.

The Earth wants to help you.
She wants to be a part of your life.
She only needs the invitation.

Let her healing energies rise through your feet.
Visualize the healing energy wrapping around your ankles, going up to your knees and thighs, twisting and turning around your organs in your belly, maneuvering around your lungs and heart, down through your arms to your fingertips, up to your throat, around your brain into your eyeballs, ears, and down the tips of your hair.
Feel the Earth's love.
It will absorb, tease out, encase, and envelop energies that do not belong, allowing you to heal and release.
Release.
Release.

Your breath is important as well.
Take slow cleansing breaths.
Breathe out that which does not belong, that which no longer serves you, and that which is to be healed. Watch these unnecessary energies flow through your feet back into the Earth.
It will be transmuted, transformed, and loved.

Loved. Loved because you are so very loved.

SPACE OUTSIDE EARTH

Today is about the space outside of Earth.
What is contained in the heavens above, the depths below, and the many stars that twinkle in the sky?

The expanse of space makes Earth seem like a grain of sand on a huge beach. Actually, it is many times smaller than that, but you get the picture.
Earth is a small planet.
I want you to know there are other grains of sand.
I want you to picture walking along this beach, splashing in the surf, letting the sand run through your fingers.

Earth is an important planet because souls come here to learn, experience, and enjoy. There are bright, vivid colors. There is much to feel and do.

Souls not only come as humans, but as animals, trees, and blades of grass.
The workings of this world have not been explained by your sciences.

Experience love, that is the purpose.
Connect, relate, enjoy, feel, and be.

PEOPLE OF EARTH

Today, we are going to talk about your journey to Earth, the people of Earth, the evolution of Earth, the continuation of Earth, and the enlightenment of Earth.

People have been on Earth for millions of years.
Humans evolved through thought, intention, and purpose.

You are not of God's image.

You are not of otherworldly beings.

You were designed for Earth, for the gravity of Earth, and with the animals of Earth.

You evolved.

You evolved consciousness.

You evolved ingenuity and humanity, and now humans are creating the destruction of humanity.

The purpose of humans on Earth was to offer a new experience for souls.

Souls are everlasting.

Souls are eternal.

Heaven is a wonderful, blissful place.

After a couple hundred thousand years of bliss, some souls desire something new and different.

There are other planets in this universe that hold intelligent life and we call those beings Intergalactics. There are some Intergalactics that have advanced technology and have helped you evolve to where you are now.

They have given you knowledge.

They have given you wisdom.

They have given you a blueprint to evolve.

Not all planets are sophisticated, but all planets are an experience.

These other planets are something to be, do, have, learn, feel, or see.

On most other planets, souls get to keep their wisdom.

They get to understand their own Akashic Record.

They understand evolution.

They understand the planet.

They understand their purpose.

They understand life, death, and how things flow and ebb throughout the Universe.

However, Earth was designed differently.

On Earth, you do not get to remember.

On Earth, you arrive having forgotten everything and needing to start from scratch.

This was to create a new experience.

Currently on Earth, humanity has chosen destitution and struggle, and because there is ultimate free will (the purpose of this planet) we must now create an environment where destitution will thrive.

However, many souls have not chosen destitution, they have chosen joy, happiness, bliss and the wonderful pleasures of humanity and humanness on Earth.

So, what do we do?

We create two worlds.

The New Earth is for souls that choose to live in high vibration.

Those who choose happiness and love for all.

Both destitution and love are desired so we must find a way to divide gracefully.

Earth is currently like oil and water that has been shaken up. There are islands of oil that are suspended in water, but eventually the oil and water will separate by continuing to move in opposite directions and in opposite flows.

Soon there will be a defined line between the two. Currently, you are still in a washing machine with islands of oil and water spinning together. Over the next 75 years or so, these two frequencies, these two choices, these two experiences of humanness will separate.

Where do you sit right now?

You are in between.

People have not learned how to evolve yet, how to use these skills, and the importance of these teachings.

How do YOU evolve?
How do YOU ascend?
How do you choose happiness?
Happiness is a choice.
A choice that can be learned.

The evolution of humans will come down to choices, beliefs, and love.

Love.
Love everyone.
Love yourself first and foremost.
Love your children.
Love your parents.
Love your neighbors.
Love every person you walk past on the street.
Love those who have done you wrong.

Forgive.
Forgive anyone and everyone.
Free your heart from any turmoil.
Always believe the best intentions for people, even if it is not what they intended, believed, or did on purpose. The point is to free YOUR heart.
This is YOUR choice.
It is your choice to be hurt.
It is your choice how you react.
It is your choice how you take people's words.

Let words roll past you if they are not kind, loving, or uplifting.
Let them breeze by, they do not need to stick.
Only take in that which lifts you up, the rest can be let go.
Live in your happiness.
Live in your joy.
Live in your freedom.

There is so much to this world.
There is so much more to being human.
There are human needs.
There is the human intellect.
There are human emotions.
There is the relationship between other humans.
There are physical needs of survival, food, shelter, and warmth.

This world was designed with a playground of experiences, a playground of emotions and bright dazzling colors. The colors of this planet are so vivid and bright!
There is so much beauty here: Flowers, trees, animals, fish, and sea life.
All these experiences add to your humanness.
But humans have forgotten their place in this world and the stewardship of the planet.

How do you support the planet?
How do you foster loving relationships with the energies and spirits of your planet, of nature, and the beings around you?
Many humans have closed themselves off to outside influences, spirits, and beings of the natural world.
You need to open this connection.
You need to walk into nature and see heart to heart the tree spirits, the flower spirits, the animals, the sunlight, and the rays floating between the trees.
These are spirits.
There are many unseen spirits to the human eye.

How do you connect?
First, you have to be open.
First, you have to allow, recognize, and be grateful.

Open your heart.
Show your love.

When you give love, you can receive love.

I encourage you to walk in the forest. Find a tree and open yourself up to that tree. Recognize it as a growing living force.
Allow yourself to feel the joy that flows within the tree.
Feel the sway of the leaves.
Feel the deep root system and feel the gifts of the tree.
To experience this, clear your mind and just be.

CHAPTER 4:
THE HUMBLE FARMER

Your connection with the Earth is still present with concrete below you. You only need to slow down to feel through the busyness.

THE HUMBLE FARMER

Today, I'm here to tell you the story of the humble farmer. He worked his land and cared for his animals and family. He was happy. He was humble, and he knew nothing else.

One day, the farmer needed to travel to a nearby village for supplies. When he arrived, the village was no longer a village – it was a busy city, a concrete jungle. He had never seen cars or glass buildings. He wandered around and saw something missing in the people bustling by. No one looked at him and no one paid attention to him.

The farmer got turned around and became lost. He wandered through the streets until he saw an elderly woman. She had gray hair, a hunched back, and walked slowly with a cane. She looked up and saw the farmer's bewilderment and said, "You look lost young man. How can I help you? What are you looking for?" In a dazed kind of way, the farmer said, "To be honest, I don't know. I came here for... I'm not sure. I am lost." She said, "I think you are lost in more ways than one. Why don't you follow me home, young man."

The farmer was unsure what to do but followed the elderly woman and helped her up the stairs to her apartment. In her apartment, she poured him some tea and they sat down at the table and began to talk.

The old woman had once been a farmer herself. She worked the land and cared for her animals. She saw something in this young farmer; she knew who he was deep inside, and what he was going through. She could see it in him. While they sat, they talked and got to know each other.

Finally, the bewilderment within the young farmer started to drift away and he realized what he came for. He had come for tools and supplies to bring back to his farm. He was unsure how long he had been there; it could have been weeks or months. As he began to regain himself, the old woman told him her story.

She was a young maiden who left home for adventure, for something different. She left her family and stumbled upon the city, where she also wandered around confused like the young farmer. Until an old woman found her and invited her in for tea. She, too, began to remember who she was and why she was there. She found a way to live in the city, but never forgot who she was. Some days she missed the farm. She missed putting her hands in the soil, she missed caring for the animals, and she missed the trees. She talked fondly of her days on the farm and the young farmer remembered how he had felt when he was at home.

Somehow, he had been blinded by the busyness around him. He had become confused, bewildered, and distracted in the busyness. Distracted from his true purpose. It turned out that he had been wandering for weeks. He was unsure where this time had gone as he had been distracted by everything.

The old woman helped him to ground himself and find his way by giving him time and care. The old woman also assisted the young farmer over the next couple days gathering what he needed. They spent time together and created a wonderful friendship. After a couple days, it was time for the farmer to head home. The old woman walked the farmer to the edge of the city, and they said goodbye. The old woman returned to her life in the city, feeling a true kinship with this farmer.

The farmer returned home with his tools and greeted his family. They were worried, but they felt in their hearts he was okay. After many months, there was a knock at the door. The young farmer opened the door to see the old woman – she had made her way to his farm. He invited her in, introduced her to everyone, and they sat down for tea. She asked if she could stay, and very happily the farmer offered her to stay as long as she wanted. The old woman worked the fields, took care of the animals, and visited the trees.

After a couple months, she returned to the farmer and said it was time for her to go back. He was confused and asked, "Why would you return to the busyness where no one sees you? Everyone is so busy and has no time to see your soul." She took his hands and said, "Because there are others like you who I must help. This is my job."

He understood and wished her well. He packed a bag with fresh cheese, apples from the trees, and goodies to send her on her way. He invited her to return any time.

The old woman walked down the path with her cane. This time, she had a renewed sense of purpose. She walked straighter and her energy was revitalized. She walked back to the city and continued her search for souls that were seeking, too distracted to see.

CHAPTER 5:
THE FUTURE IS LOVE

Love is the only human emotion that lifts your soul above the human plane.

GOD IS A CONSCIOUSNESS

The current understanding of God is as a being, yet I am not a being.

I am a consciousness.

Much like the human consciousness, but more of the world and the universe, and on a greater scale.

I'm not one being.

I am many beings.

I am any and all beings.

I am also the Universe.

I am also a planet.

I am also human.

I am everything.

Everything flows through me: All life, all death, all matter.

I am the eternal consciousness – the consciousness of the future, of the past, and of the present.

I am also energy, light, and matter.

I am time.

There is not yet a conceptual understanding of what I am, but eventually it will be shown, proven, quantitated, and be tangible for those to feel, see, and understand.

Until that time, there is faith.

A faith of belief.

A faith of caring.

A faith of love because that is what I truly am: Love.

I am a consciousness of love.

There are high frequencies.

There are low frequencies.

There cannot be one without the other.

They balance each other, so I am both.

How can this be, you ask. How could this not be, I ask.

How can there not be a yin without the yang.

Look towards quantum mechanics for rudimentary answers. There is not yet the science and technology developed to show in this present day, but it will come.

We are energy.

We are energetic beings.

Look to the smallest molecules within you, the smallest entities, parts of entities, parts of beings, part of atoms.

You are energy.

You control the energy with your life force.

I am on a greater scale, but of the same.

So, find your light.

Find your purpose.

Find what you want in life.

Project it into the future, wrap your mind around it, and see yourself there.

That is how you get what you want – is to create it.

You must align your vibrational frequency to that which you are wanting.

If your physical actions and intentions are not in alignment, you cannot attain what you wish.

To attain what you wish, you must believe.
You must feel.

You must be.

Allow yourself to be happy, to be joyful, and to invite in love.
Invite in that which makes you happy and release that which does not.

ASCENSION OF SOULS

Today will be about your soul's journey, Serraphine.
Your journey started billions of years ago with the creation of this universe.

You lived many lives on a water planet, surrounded by water beings, living in a collective unit. This collectivity taught you about energy flow, movement, grace, and balance. There was not a lot of high thinking on this planet, so you outgrew it and went to a sand world.

The sand worlds had blue pools of water but were mostly sand. The beings there lived a small life, but had a higher consciousness, higher thinking, and critical thinking.

Next, you evolved to a highly intelligent planet and there you spent many lifetimes. While there, you developed integrity, worth, and growth.
While there, you ascended to a higher being, an enlightened being.
You chose others over yourself.
You chose spiritual growth.

You chose intellectual growth.
In that world, you became enlightened.
You dedicated your life to ascension.

Ascension of souls – what does this mean?
When a soul ascends, it has crossed through to a new vibrational level.
(Vibrational levels being conscious and unconscious.)
Once the ceiling was broken for your soul, you had more opportunities, and more complex dimensional thought processes.
You carried with you all your lifetimes and lessons and brought these wisdoms with you to Earth.

You first came as a spiritual teacher.
You came to teach, before the time of teaching, before the Awakening.
You laid the groundwork.
You laid the vibrational process.
You have lived multiple lives here on Earth – most have been consumed with laying the foundation of the work that you do now.
There is a framework that was put into place, not only by you, but by many others who came to Earth knowing the true purpose, the true possibilities of what this planet holds.

How is it possible we sit here and talk?
How is it possible that you are a portal between two worlds?
How is it possible to bring a coherent message?

These lifetimes taught you many facets of humanity.
The many facets of humanity trickle down like a waterfall.
You come here today to grow that waterfall; to take it from a stream into a raging river.

The message you bring is of hope, love, and joy.

This message is created for the masses.
This message is created with love, with endless abounding love.

Embrace this gift.
Embrace this life.
Embrace all that you have and all you bring.

Life here on Earth is not simple; it is quite complicated.
It is complicated in the depth of emotion that humans feel.
It is complicated in the survival and elements that are required:
Food, hunger, shelter, politics, relationships, and money.
There is a complex level of thinking that must be attained for a successful life.

There is also Ego.
Ego has reshaped the planet, not only energetically but physically as well.
The planet is sick, and she hurts, and ego prevents us from healing her.
Ego and the pursuit of money, greed, and selfishness.

But do not fear.
Know you are taken care of.
You are provided for, and there is a path into the light.
This path is spread before you and everyone.
You have free will.

You are creator beings, so create!

Create this new world.
Create this eternal bliss.
Create the New Earth.

The New Earth is for Ascended Beings, for Enlightened Ones, and for those who choose to be.
It does not matter what belief system you carry, what nationality

you are, how you grew up; it is your vibrational level that matters.
It is your choice the level you vibrate at.

Your thoughts determine this.

The New Earth is for all and anyone who chooses.

This is for everyone.

THE FUTURE IS LOVE

Today is about the future – what will be, what is to come, and how to get there.

The future is love.

The future is joy.

The future is peace – an unwavering peace.

It is an unwavering love – for each other, for the planet, and for everything.

This evolution has happened many times before – not with Earth, but with other ascended beings. We are creating multi-dimensional life forms. You already are a multi-dimensional being, but we are creating another reality inversion. This version in the future, will be able to ascend time.

What does it mean to ascend time? you just asked.

There are multiple aspects to ascending time – you can be in more than one place at one time, you can quantumly jump between times, you can move your thoughts through space to connect with another person.

This multi-dimensional communication, being, and thought process will all be learned.

Know this is who you are and who you were intended to be.

This connection between the human consciousness will be developed more in time.

You will learn how to tap into and access this information. You will learn how to communicate, to transmit information, to gather information and to move through time and space – not in the sense you currently understand (think more Willy Wonka). This change in matter, quantum physics, and dynamics has not yet evolved, but it is coming.

Currently, you need to focus on love.
You need to focus on the vibration of love and have that be your personal vibration.
It is the highest vibrational level that you can ascend to.
Love for yourself and every living being.

Accept others no matter what.
Show others love.
Show others kindness.
Show others forgiveness.
Show others the way because there is only love.

The other emotions of humanness are choices.
They are versions of ego, and it is time for them to be released.
Release them and let them go.
Shed them off because as you ascend, you will learn they truly do not matter.
They are not part of who you are as a soul, and they will not bring you happiness.

If you choose to live this lifetime in happiness, then this is the way forward:
Live in gratitude.
Live in harmony.
Live in reverence.
Live in love.
Love is all around you.

Love is being emitted by the forest, trees, rocks, and other animals.

They live in love.

They live in peace.

Tap into the vibration of the forest.

Take yourself on a walk and listen to the trees. They will speak to you on the wind.

Let the winds come, let the ground soak in your emotions.

Give Mother Earth your emotions, she will transmute it into something beautiful.

That is what she does, she transfers energy.

She does not understand good or bad in the sense you do.

She can change it into love.

This is a very special gift your Earth has.

Speak with the ocean.

Listen to her song.

The sound of the waves, the constant rhythm is her music.

Let it lull you and speak to you.

Let it sink into your soul.

Ground yourself with the Earth.

Lift yourself up to the Moon and expand everywhere in between.

You have the capability, and you will learn.

Allow yourself to be free.

Free from the programmed ego, programmed family issues, and programmed nonsense.

Only live within what makes you happy.

If it does not make you happy, let it go.

Let it go.

Realize that you are a creator being, so you create the life around you.

If you let something go, then you can bring in more joy and happiness.
You have made more room.

What does your new life look like?
Create the picture in your mind.
Create the beautiful world and life that you will have, because this is what your life can be.

You must release all other emotions because these emotions are what you are creating.
If you focus on the negative, then you are creating the negative.
If you focus on the positive, then you are creating the positive.

Know that this will take time, and that is OK.
You can change your mind to find what suits you best.
Hone it in.
Feel it.
Live it.
Pull it towards you.
You can create anything!
Anything you desire!

You may have to work to get there.
You may have to unload many suitcases of baggage but continue walking towards that dream.
Define the dream.
Picture the dream.
Live in the dream and it will come.
It will come.

If you live your day-to-day life in happiness, in gratitude, with forgiveness, in joy, and peace, that is what you create into the future.
That is the life that you will walk.

Own that love.
Own that peace.
Make it fully incorporated into who you are, and release everything else.

You place masks upon your face as a learned protection mechanism.
These masks can be taught by your families, your culture, your childhood, or anytime you are unsure how to navigate in the human world.
Sometimes when masks are created, you lose part of yourself.
As you move forward in love, ask that all pieces be returned to you whole and healed.

Move forward into your happiness.
Regain your soul.
Regain your life's purpose.
Regain all possibilities!

That is the gift of humanity.
That is the gift of Earth.
Be true to yourself.
Be true to the being that you are.
An eternal being, living a human experience.
Enjoy it and have fun! That is part of the reason you came to Earth.

THE PEOPLE TO COME

Today, we are going to talk about the people to come.
People as you know them will evolve.
They will evolve into Master Beings, Master Beings of Light, humanity, and evolution.

They will find technologies for good.

They will heal all disease and all wounds.

The human body will ascend to be a Temple of Light, a Temple of Spirit, and a Temple of Experience.

You will be able to walk between worlds.

You will be able to experience humanity, but will also experience collectivity, unconditional love, and a knowingness about each other.

You call it empathy now, but it will be how people will communicate in the future.

There will be a mind-to-mind connection and an ability to look into someone's energetic field.

This technology is not that far off.

You already do it now, but you do not understand how to use it.

It will be learned, it will be honed, it will be challenged, but ultimately that will be the progression. There will be information downloaded into the human unconscious mind that will allow this to happen.

The evolution of humans was always meant to take this course.

The divergence of worlds was not intended.

However, for humans to ascend to the beings they are meant to be, this divide must happen.

There was a hope for all humanity to evolve into Enlightened Beings, but it has become evident that is not possible. Actually, you were on the brink of destruction.

Those who choose enlightenment will move forward in a graceful glide, while the other world slips down into darkness.

Ascend into the light and feel unconditional love, joy, and being supported.

This world is hard enough without ego and the social pressures that are experienced now. Live your life in love, in joy, in friendships, in loving relationships, supported in collective union and in nourishment.

Your hearts will speak to one another.
Your minds will see each other,
Your souls will understand one another.
Embrace this love to be.

CHAPTER 6:
TIME OF CHANGE

*Let love be your guiding light
in the darkest time of your life.*

DARK LANDS

Once upon a time, there was a dark land with dark waters, dark clouds, dark mountains, and dark seas with waves that lapped upon the shore.

Black sand made its way up into the hills.

The hills were covered in ash, soot, and death.

This darkness covered and stretched many miles into the land before there were semblances of life.

Inland, there were trees and small shrubs.

Even farther inland, there were animals and multifaceted life.

This barren land was caused by disease.

Disease and anger consumed the life force.

The life force could no longer thrive, so it moved into the ground.

These emotions are the lowest on the vibrational scale: Anger, hate, frustration, hurt, and jealousy.

This spectrum of energy, vibration, emotion, thrives not only within humans, but is also present within the planet.

You are vibrational beings.

Your cells resonate, vibrate, and communicate.

This low-energy form arrived with human consciousness.
Humans allowed this to grow.
Humans fostered and encouraged it.

This is where we are at now.

What happens to this Earth?
What happens to this land, sea, and sky that are no longer vital?
Everything changes.
Everything evolves.
There will be darker beings.

However, those who choose a higher vibrational life – filled with vitality, happiness, joy, peace, love – those who choose love, those who choose forgiveness, and those who choose to evolve will grow.

They are drawn into the woods, into the energies that are similar to and resonate within them.
They will be sheltered, allowed to bloom, and allowed to grow.
When this happens, the world evolves.
The world will change.
The world will bloom and divide.

In this division, there will be two human worlds on different energetic planes.
Right now, these energetic frequencies are within the same physical plane, yet they are energetically separate. It will take many generations for the actual physical separation to take place.

There will be a higher good.
There will be a higher ascension, a higher consciousness, and evolution.

Those who wish to come to Earth to experience difficulty will still be drawn to this other world. Within time, humans will evolve or implode, but this evolution will create a higher being, and a higher consciousness.

You must separate from lower frequencies and the intensity of the lower frequencies to move into a higher consciousness.
That which is being weighed down will break away and you will continue to progress.

Have faith.
Live in love.
Embrace those around you.
Feel happy.
Feel joy.
Feel peace and love.
Love to all. All there really is, is love. Embrace this.

POLES OF LOVE & DESPAIR

There is much turmoil in the world you live in.
There is fear and chaos winding around you.
This unfortunately eats at your soul.
Eats at your mind and raises guilt within you.
It is hard to watch those around you suffer.

There are growing pockets of deep love.
This love is reaching deeper and deeper into a person's soul.
Love is divine.
Love is effervescent throughout one's soul.
Love is all-encompassing and all healing.
The love you feel for yourself, your family, community and the world is growing deeper.

You see the extremes.

You feel the love.

The love grows deeper in your heart, yet you watch the suffering expand.
You see poverty and struggle, and yet you experience life differently.
You are untouched by this other world that exists around you.
It does not touch you.

You choose a different path.
You choose love.
You choose happiness and joy.
You choose to learn, expand, and grow.
You choose the light.
You choose your vibration.

Your vibration is attached to your thoughts.
Your thoughts are chosen by you.
Therefore, your frequency is chosen by you.

The only difference between you and those living in despair is vibration.
You can choose to be where they are, and they can choose to be where you are.
You have that choice.
That choice is within everyone.

You only need the tools and the wisdom.
Allow yourself to be happy.
Allow yourself to feel joy, gratitude, and elation.
This is part of your human experience.
You are here to feel love.
You are here to be human.
To live a joyous life.

I want this for everyone on the planet.
I want them all to be happy and to do that, they need tools.

They need information on how to do this, how to transition, how to move their life in the direction they want.

It sounds so simple, and honestly, it is simple.
Unfortunately, there is family and social conditioning that must be undone.

It is a choice – a choice to move into joy.

I want everyone to move into joy.
I want everyone to feel the Divine Love pouring into this planet.
I want to deepen the wells of love, the oceans and currents of love, that fall upon you.

How does this happen?
Thoughts, vibration, love, and acceptance.

How do you tap into this?
Start by turning inward and loving yourself.

Change your inner voice to be one that lifts you up
and shows you what you can be.
Allows you to dream.
Allows you to dream so big you can be anything.
You are so much more than a physical body.

You are a spiritual being with divine energy flowing through you.
You are connected to everything.
The more you work on your own energy and vibration,
the more you ripple out amongst all people to bring up the collective energy.

Things are growing in each direction, and with that we need balance.
Those who are in the deepest of despair are balanced by those deeply attuned to love and joy.

These two opposites are pulling away from each other.
The poles are getting farther and farther apart.

These two worlds on one planet do not touch, yet they are in the same physical plane.
Eventually, in time this will change.
Things will separate in the physical plane as well.

You, my child, are here to bring the pole of love deeper and further away from the pole of despair.
This will happen with collective energy.
This will happen with knowledge.
This will happen with new vibrations that are exposed, allowed, and accepted into the planet, into this Earth's physical plane.

CHAPTER 7:
PURSUIT OF HAPPINESS

*Money will not buy you freedom,
you must find it in your mind.*

PURSUIT OF HAPPINESS

Today, we have a story of a young man who sought fame, fortune, and financial gain. The ways of the world taught him to value this and taught him that is what he should seek.

He aspired to be famous because he thought that was love.
He thought that was accomplishment.
He thought this was what he was supposed to dream.
He worked hard throughout his life and hurt many people along the way.

When he was older, he laid on his yacht thinking about his life and the emptiness he felt inside.
The emptiness within his heart, the loneliness, even though people were around him.
As he laid in the sun, he thought about what he could have done differently.

The life he could have had.

A young server came by and asked if he wanted anything. The gentleman told the young man to sit down and asked, "Are you truly happy with your life?"

The server was taken aback and thought for a moment. He replied, "Yes, I believe my life is happy." The wealthy gentleman asked him, "Why? Why do you feel happy? What is so right with your life?"

The young man thought about his life and smiled, then said, "My wife is the kindest person I know. We have two beautiful children who are healthy, happy, and thriving. I have wonderful parents and siblings, and we enjoy the time we spend together. We have family meals. We have extended get-togethers regularly and my family makes me happy."

The wealthy man sat back then asked, "Why do you serve me? Why do you come on this yacht and do what I ask?" The server replied, "I'm only away from my family every once in a while. You do not live on this yacht, but when you are sailing, I get to see the world. I get to appreciate my family and understand what I'm missing. I miss them and we have joyous reunions when I come home."

The wealthy gentleman dismissed the server and stared up at the sky thinking. *I have family but it is not a joyous occasion when we get together. I don't think highly of my wife, my children, my siblings, or my parents.*

He was frustrated and began to look at his life differently. If this young man felt he was happy serving someone else and living a modest life, why in his grandeur was he miserable? He began to dissect his life and peel away the layers of what he had and what this young man had said.

He took apart the conversation in an analytical way, which gave him answers that were somewhat lacking. He realized that when he was around his family it was not a joyous occasion; instead, it was analytical and critical. It was about accomplishments and conquering, rather than joy. He sought to change this one thing.

When his family gathered, he made an effort to make it a joyous occasion: To change the subject, to reroute conversations, to think about things differently. He found that in a couple weeks, things began to change, attitudes began to shift, and there was a happiness that began to emerge when they were together.

He decided he was onto something. He thought about what the young man said about freedom and appreciation for his family while he was away. The wealthy man began to change his inner dialog – how he considered his family and how he considered his happiness.

He found as he continued to do this work that money did not mean as much anymore. It was still nice to have pretty things, freedom, and to be able to travel and explore the world, but he recognized a pressure that weighed on him. Not only was he putting pressure on himself, but the world was putting pressure on him with expectations, with an oppressive force he sought to get out from under.

It took years for the wealthy man to change his thoughts and change his interactions with people. He found he was now much healthier, happier, and grateful.

A couple years later while sailing on his yacht, the same server was there so he pulled him aside to say, "I want to thank you for your honesty with me, and the lessons that you were able to communicate. I've taken many of these into my heart, put them into action, and it has made a big difference. Thank you." The server was surprised, and he told the wealthy man he was grateful and that he was happy for him.

The wealthy man continued his quest to learn, to grow, to be grateful, and to live in a life of happiness, removing the pressures put upon him by others and himself.

He realized they do not truly make him happy. He was the only one who could make himself happy, with his thoughts, with his love, and with his gratitude.

Part 2

THE AWAKENING PROCESS

CHAPTER 8:
CHANGES WITHIN

You contain the knowledge of the universe inside each of your cells. By connecting inward, you expand greater outward.

THE SPACE IN BETWEEN

The beyond.
Earth.
The space in between.

The space in between has many meanings.
It has many meanings in a large and a small sense.
In the large sense, you can think of outer space and planets.
In the small sense, you can think of atoms and electrons.

The space in between the electrons – you do not have a great name for that presently; however, as technology develops you will find this is where consciousness lives.
This is where the life force is, and this is where we work.
As technology grows, so will your understanding of what the space in between is, how it works, and how it can be influenced.
You must be careful because it can be controlled, and right now you have some disruptors that you need to be careful of.
All the electronic mechanisms you have around you can disrupt

this space.

Understand that you are an energetic being.

I know I've said that many times, but what is an energetic being?

Energy flows through you constantly, with every thought, muscle movement, or twitch.

You have an electrical pulse running through you.

This electrical pulse creates an energy field.

This energy field is affected by the electrical twitches and thoughts you have in your brain. The thoughts you have create a cascading effect throughout your body.

It not only affects the energetic synapses, but it also affects the space in between.

The life force that you carry can have impressions placed upon it and absorbed into it.

These impressions can leave a devastating effect,

or it can leave a wonderful effect.

That is why you need to live in love.

That is why, as an energetic being, to live successfully on Earth – pain-free, disease-free and with a clear-thinking mind for an entire lifetime – you need good energetic health.

That is not a concept that has been talked about yet, or understood, or the gravity of it taken into consideration.

There is much to come.

There is much technology to come.

There is much wisdom to come, and it will also show how to clear these energetic imprints on your space in between.

Technology will get there; it is only time.

HEALING WITHIN

Let's discuss the New Earth.

The New Earth is a place of bliss, a place of community, and a place of freedom.

Freedom in a way that is not understood.

Freedom to be who you truly are.

Freedom to pursue what you truly desire.

Freedom to look inside and love the person you are and know that as you express yourself and what makes you happy, everyone is there to support you.

Everyone is there to help you because you are there to help them.

There is a support system, love, and gratefulness for everyone's contributions.

There is a community that is free flowing with thoughtforms, with activities, and with duty.

People are grateful to do the work that needs to get done, and opportunities are open to everyone.

The freedoms you understand now are not truly freedoms in your world. They are luxuries of being born to the right families and the right circumstance.

Freedom can be a thought form, an expression of yourself, pursuit of a career or education, or access to education.

Freedom can be access to new thought forms.

This community is self-sustaining.

This community has evolved technology and is sustainable.

The Earth is supported and loved, and her needs are also met. She is not depleted in the ways she is now. She is an integral part of this system. There is an understanding of the roles that humans are meant to play. An understanding of the balance between nature, energy, humans, and all life. There is meant to be a symbiotic relationship, a harmony.

Currently, there is disease, there is pain, and there is imbalance. As the New Earth continues to form and progress, more balance will start to take place.
This may take a bit of time, but the technology and the availability of the technology – with the ability to balance – will continue to move with the New Earth.
There is unlimited technology that is to come.
This technology will expand not only the human mind but the human ability.

The symbiotic relationship will be expanded to include not only animals and Earth, but also yourself.
You have symbiotic relationships within you.
You think of your organs as being part of you, as being a contributor to how your body works, but there is an independence as well and there is an identity. In disease, the way you think of it now, there is an imbalance when something does not work properly. It is also understanding that balance and symbiosis need to work within all parts within yourself. If there is a disease within one organ, it affects the entire body because the body cannot function properly.

So, how do you get the organ back in harmony with the whole body?
You will learn how energetically this can happen.
You will learn how to listen to organs, how to listen to your body, and how to explore the relationships you have with the systems within your body.

The systems within the human body are just a microcosm of what is occurring on Earth, what is occurring in nature.

It is a microcosm of the imbalance that is happening on your planet.

We need to get everything back into harmony.

How do we get everything back into harmony?
How do you support an organ that does not have the function it needs?
One, you need to identify what is going on, what is the cause for the imbalance?
Is there an energy imbalance?
Is there a negative thought form?
Is there hurt, shame, and/or blame that has been taken on by this organ?
There could also be other causes, but we will simplify here.

An organ may take the emotional pain the body feels.
This emotional pain was created by the thoughts and thought forms of the mind.
The mind created a thought pattern.
The mind created a thought pattern which created energy, which then needed to go somewhere and be expressed, but it was not. So, the organ has taken on this energy. It has become the dumping ground for all the negative thoughts.

Identify the thoughts in your mind, the unhealthy patterns, and rewrite and rewire the pain and hurt, and move into release, forgiveness, happiness, joy, and abundance.
Use all the tools you have available to you.

The first step is recognition and identification.
Once it is identified, it can be released, and you can choose whether to keep the thoughts and the patterns.

Once thought patterns are changed, negative energy is no longer being collected in the organ, and the organ may begin to heal. It can purge and it can release if you ask. If you are willing to do the work.

As it releases, it needs support.

This is only one example of healing the body and oneself.
This metaphor needs to be expanded to the Earth, to societies, and to families where the same patterns and changing of thoughts need to happen.

Loving oneself is where to start.
Forgiving yourself.
Allowing yourself to be happy.
Allowing yourself to be free.

Allowing yourself to find what brings you joy.

Find your joy and live in it.
Find your gratitude and thank it.

LIGHTNING FORMS

Today is about lightning.
Lightning is a phenomenon that occurs when the skies create an electrical charge.
An electrical charge that builds and must be released and then plummets to the Earth.

THE LIGHT WITHIN

Today, I would like to talk about the light within.

The light within.
The light within everyone.

The glowing torch that connects and enlightens.

This glowing torch is a life force within all of us.

It is the life force that animates the human body -that creates thoughts, movements, dreams, and imagination.

You are more than connections and wires, and by that, I mean you are more than nerves, hormones, and synapses.

You are more than that; there is a consciousness within each of your cells.

They know how to communicate and can communicate their desires.

The consciousness and a knowingness are within every cell and within every organ.

It lives in the space in between.

The space in between, you ask, "What does this mean?"

The space between atoms.

The space between the electrons, the neutrons, and the protons.

You will find when you go beyond this level that this is where your consciousness lives – where this knowingness and aliveness take place.

Your science will soon prove this, but until that day, know that this is where you are found.

You envelop and embrace so much more than your brain.

You have a knowingness inside your fingers and toes, and it radiates from you, creating what many would call your aura.

Your aura is an electrical field that radiates from you.

This electrical field can feel your surroundings and know your surroundings.

It interprets your surroundings and other people.

It is time to learn how to use these gifts – how to expand beyond your physical body into your electrical field.

Once you learn to expand your knowingness and consciousness

beyond the physical form, you will be able to do so much more.
You will be able to walk into another's field and communicate gracefully without words.
You will be able to feel other beings, your pets, and the trees and communicate with them easily.

Once you see beyond yourself, both figuratively and literally,
you will change and you will evolve.
To move your consciousness beyond yourself, there are learned ways,
but first you need to break free of the egoic thought processes.
You need to break free from self-limiting thoughts.
You must break free from your mind and know you are so much more than your mind.
Your mind is limiting you; it is not the source of your knowingness.

The source of your knowingness is your consciousness.
Learn how to expand your consciousness.
Learn how to expand your knowingness.
Tap into the world that is around you, and you will see it with more than just your eyes.

Feel the love, feel the joy, and feel the oneness that is around you.

THE AWAKENING

Let's discuss the moment of change.
The moment of change is the moment your cells wake up.
The moment your inner light shines.
The moment that your consciousness ascends to a new level.

The waking of the light that is within will be immediate for some and gradual for others. Those who are ready can awaken quickly; they can walk into their new life, melt away the old roadblocks, and move forward into a life of freedom. The roadblocks that seemed so big and daunting before suddenly melt away and seem small – seem so insignificant.

The thought forms that held you back are no longer there. Or if they are, they seem trivial.

The awakening within is an important milestone for your soul.
It is an important milestone for society.
It is an important milestone for your consciousness.

This is the time of mass awakening; it is time for people to wake up.
It is time for people to move forward into the light.
Seek a new life.
Seek a life of purpose.
Seek a life that is rewarding, not only monetarily, but deep in your soul.

Allow the awakening to take place.
It is simple.
First, you must desire to awaken.
You must desire Awakening within your soul, within the essence of yourself,
deep in your consciousness, your soul, your spirit.
You must ask for this awakening.
It must be your free will, and it must be your calling.
Ask and it will happen.

There are simple hand movements that when traced along your chakras, awaken a light within you.
This dormant light has been waiting for this time.
It is within all humans who desire to become enlightened.

The awakening process will not only change you, your mind, and your consciousness, it will change your cells also.

It will change the way your cells communicate.

It will change the knowingness within your cells.

It will change your aura.

It will change the electrical synapses inside your brain because they will be bathed in a new light and a new energy.

A light from the heavens will shine down upon you and bathe, cleanse, and clear your soul, allowing the roadblocks that seemed so significant to melt away.

Allow this process to happen within you.

Recognize the Awakening Process and see it for what it is: Your transition, your awakening, and your enlightenment.

Enlightenment is a grand time.

It is an exciting time.

There is so much more to come.

There is so much more to this human life.

Enlightenment will awaken your senses.

It will awaken your abilities.

It will awaken your transcendence.

As you awaken, you will open your soul

and as your soul feels the light, it will connect.

It will connect in a new way to others who are awake.

You will see the light within them.

You will see their radiance.

You will understand them on a new level.

The awakening process has three phases.

For some, all three will be completed at once.

Others will have work that must be done at each phase.

Each phase will open a door – a door to your consciousness, which causes your awakening and vibrational fields to shift.

You must be ready for this, and you must release things that are holding you back.

The process will bring clarity to what those changes will be.

Once you understand what is happening and what is shifting, you will have a greater understanding of the New Earth, human consciousness, and the true abilities of humans.

You are so much more than beings walking on this planet.

There is so much more to this planet.

There is so much more to this universe.

There is so much more that you can connect to once you are awake.

The first step is to ask and have the desire.

Seek the hand motions of the awakening activation.

Find the truth you are seeking inside yourself.

Allow the changes to happen, and then sink into them.

Fall into them.

Feel yourself changing.

Feel yourself growing your energetic field.

Growing your awareness.

Growing your being.

Once these changes start falling into place,

Once you awaken and start to grow beyond your physical form,

the second phase will be to connect and understand that we are all one.

You will be able to reach out beyond your mind and connect with those around you, the planet, all humans, all animals, all beings, all consciousnesses.

Connect with those around you.

Connect with your pets at home.

Connect with trees, plants, grass, rocks, the sky, the moon, and

the stars.
You will move beyond yourself to become so much more.

The third phase will come in time and will be about collectivity.
The energy that is created in this transition will call others to you,
creating a collective energetic unit.

You do not need to be in the same city to be able to build upon the
energetic changes that are happening within you.
Time and space become irrelevant.
You are a multidimensional being.
You will learn how to transcend space, time, and matter.

Create communities and connect.
Create online forums.
Create supportive units.
Get together, talk, share your experiences because you are
creating a collective.
The energy of bringing people together to share experiences will
propel this forward.
Find like-minded people.

Because of the changes that are happening within you,
you will find that what you once sought for – happiness – may
not be the same.
You may grow in different ways.
You may seek different things.
Find support.
Find connection.
You were never meant to be solitary.
You were meant to support one another.
You are meant to be collective.
Find your support system and find your like-minded companions.

Grow this energy together and as you do, it will start radiating.

People will be called to this; people will be called to you and will ask you what you have done. They will want to know what is different about you.

They won't necessarily know and recognize the light that is now shining bright within you, but they will feel it.
They will know in their unconscious mind that something is different.
You seem happier and more radiant.
Share willingly and openly.
This will become a common dialog.
Share and embrace those who are going through change.
Embrace those who are seeking happiness.
Embrace those who are so much more than this human life because you have awakened.

You have transcended.
Your consciousness has bloomed and has evolved.
Share and Love.
Love those around you.
Love those who choose to take this path and love those who choose not to.
You must honor free will.
You must rise above and recognize your happiness is not the same as anyone else's, and that is okay because you love unconditionally.
You love endlessly and unbound.
Let your love shine.

THE CHANGES WITHIN

The changes within have begun to shift and adjust.
The changes within are profound.

The changes within when it happens may feel like nothing or may feel like everything.
Just because your experience is not the same as the person beside you, does not mean it is not significant.

You will be given teachings in your time.
You will be shown the way in your time.
You will also have the path opened to you in your time.

You must understand this: Everything we do is on the universal scale, and we honor your free will because we are divine beings.
We honor your sovereignty.
We honor the choices you made for this life.
We are delighted you would like to take this journey with us.
We love you unconditionally if you choose not to.

As the changes progress within your body,
after the light has erupted from within,
your cells change communication.
Your cells will purge the darkness and the denser energy forms.
This may be uncomfortable for a time depending on your situation.
For some this will be easy.
For others this may be difficult and longer.
Nonetheless, you will all progress and move forward into the light;
you will all move forward into the streaming sunshine that is waiting for you.

This light that is now shining within you is not only your light, your consciousness, and your energy, it is the universe, the consciousness of the universe, and a connection to everyone and everything.

As you envelop the light into every cell and every part of you, changes and shifts will happen.

Your thoughts will change, your desires may change, and the depth of happiness you are able to feel will change.

Lower levels of vibration will be cut off and the deep despair you possibly once felt will no longer be available to you because those vibrations are no longer available on the New Earth.

You have stepped your foot forward on the path of the New Earth. As you are on that path moving forward, moving into the light, moving into joy, moving into the collective union, you are leaving parts of your old life behind.

See this as a beautiful thing.

See this as growth.

See this as the new you – the new happy you.

The changes within will be profound.

The changes within will not stop there.

As you seek community, the changes will continue to expand.

As you seek support, the collective energy will grow.

As the changes progress, you will be faced with choices, and you will be faced with decisions.

You will also be faced with realities – realities of choices you have made in the past, and of decisions you made that hurt others.

You must make peace within. You must forgive.

Forgive yourself and forgive others.

Allow the energies, the thoughts, and the hurt to flow through you.

Allow them to be lessons.

Allow them to be part of what created who you are today.

Allow them to be honored, thanked, and gracefully placed
into the Earth,
into the fire,
into the ocean,
into the wind.

Release them and let them go.
They were an important part of how you got here today,
and possibly without these painful lessons,
you would not have sought these teachings.

The road to this lesson, to this teaching, will be different for everyone.
The Awakening process will be different for everyone.

Honor that.
Know that your journey, your awakening is special to you, and must be honored for what you are experiencing.
What others are experiencing does not matter, it is not your process.
It is theirs and they must honor their teaching, lessons, pain, and release just as you.

We must forgive our families,
forgive our societies,
forgive our world leaders.
They do not know any better. They are caught up in this egoic world that has taught them how to behave. You must forgive them.
Forgive yourself for any contribution you had.

Now that you are awake, you can make different choices.
Now that you are awake, you are a different person.
Not only in your mind, but in your physical body, your energetic body, and your spiritual body.

Recognize the difference and recognize the two versions of you.
The awakened you, who is aware and who knowingly makes choices for the betterment of your life, your family's life, for your community's life, your society's life, and for the world.

Anything that happened in the past is forgiven and honored for bringing you to this moment.

Remember this moment in time.

Remember where you are.

Remember how you feel.

Remember, grow, and see how far you have come.

Reflect and be grateful.

Be grateful for this physical body that has brought you here to this moment.

It has allowed you to expand into the cosmos because that is where you are going.

That is where this will lead.

That is what is to come.

Embrace the excitement.

Embrace the love and embrace the change.

LIGHTNING GROWS

Lighting streaks across the sky.

Electrical charges build within the clouds.

The release, the power, and the strike.

The phenomenon of lightning is one of Earth's most powerful.

Lightning shoots across the sky, transforming the electrical field within the clouds.

Changing, mystifying, and grounding.

Connecting the Earth to the clouds, and to the beings above.

The radiance of the clouds and the sky.

A shifting of atoms and particles.

*AWAKENING ACTIVATION

The Awakening Process.
The actual awakening process is very simple.
The complicated part is having people understand what they are asking for.

Ultimately, you are asking for your soul to connect to universal oneness, and for the enlightenment process to begin.
This activation option was created to jump start the enlightenment movement, the mass awakening that is needed to propel the New Earth forward.

The steps for someone to awaken through this process will be simple:
You must move your hand over your 3rd Eye, down to the Throat Chakra and over the Heart Chakra.
You must ask for connection and enlightenment during this phase.
The enlightenment process is beautiful and uplifting.

Take a couple deep breaths and allow yourself to feel grounded into the Earth.
Feel your feet connect deep into the Earth's core.

I want you to picture your Crown Chakra opening.

I want you to picture a beautiful lotus flower twisting to allow the center to be exposed.
The beautiful flower is welcoming in the divine light.
Keep your focus on your Crown Chakra, picture the beautiful flower there, hovering a couple inches above the top of your head.

Now I want you to picture a divine light.

A divine, loving, beautiful light; a light from the heavens.

Repeat after me:
"I invite in the divine light of love.
I invite in the Universal Consciousness.
I invite in unconditional love and joy.
I invite the change that will begin within me.
I allow this process to move me forward into the New Earth,
into the Oneness.
I welcome this light, this joy, and ask that it provide healing,
forgiveness, and grace."

*Now picture the light above, the light of the universe, the divine light,
the universal light, coming in through the flower above your head into
your Crown Chakra.*
It enters through your Crown Chakra, into your body.
*Place your thumb over your Third Eye, and move your thumb slowly
down your nose, mouth and neck to your Throat Chakra.*
Watch the light travel down your body following your thumb.

The light is now at your Throat Chakra.
*Continue to move your thumb down to your heart, to your breastbone
and push gently.*
Feel the light join your Heart Chakra.
Keep pressure there.

Now place your hand gently on your belly.
*Feel the light continue to move gently down through your body and the
rest of your chakras.*

*If you are sitting, the light will move through your sacrum bone into
the Earth. If you are standing, it will start to travel down both legs into
the Earth, connecting the universal light from above, through you,
into the Earth.*
Feel the light move through you, gently awakening all your cells.

Sit quietly and allow yourself to bathe in this new light.

Feel it fill you.
Feel the peace it brings.
Feel the calm.
Feel the connectedness with the Earth and with Source.

LIGHTNING STRIKES

Lightning has crashed.
Lightning erupts in the sky, connecting the heavens and the Earth by a giant bolt of energy and of light.
The light erupts from the sky and strikes upon the Earth;
a massive energetic force has arrived.
Lightning has struck every one of you who chooses to move forward with awakening.
Picture the light, the force, and the power of a lightning bolt going through you into the Earth.
That is the force that the light from above has arrived with.

CHAPTER 9:
PHASES OF AWAKENING

The dreams inside your mind are your soul whispering her desires.

THE NEW EARTH IS UPON US

The time of the New Earth is upon us.

It is the time of Enlightenment.

As you wake up, reality begins to shift.

The reality that was once the darkness of Earth, of society, will no longer be.

You will move to a reality where everything is possible, where happiness thrives, where those around you see possibility and open doors for you rather than close them.

This new reality is the reality of living a life that has endless possibilities, that has support and love flowing around them.

This is what is waiting for you and what is available to you.

Embrace the steps that are to come.

Embrace the joy and the connectedness.

Once your physical body sheds the densities, the disease, the pain, the discomfort, you will be born anew.

Your cells are bathed in a new light, and they will begin to function optimally.

Remember, you always have free will.

You can choose to go back to the Old Earth,

to bring pain back to you, and to continue negative thought patterns.

You can always go back.

This is not a one-time chance.

This door is open to you, always and forever.

Many people may choose to go back because the process to the New Earth is uncomfortable and unknown to them.

That is okay.

However, many will choose to move forward quickly and smoothly, because it is what they have chosen.

Once the body sheds the densities, you are free.

You will have a freedom that you never understood before –

shaking off the constructs of society's expectations, blooming a new idea of self within you.

You will experience a new idea of possibilities, and a new idea of who you are.

Be gentle with yourself as you explore this new version of you, this new version of possibilities.

Find your happiness.

Create a dream within your head, within your imagination.

Build an entire world where you live that dream.

Write it down.

Draw pictures.

Create, because you are creator beings, and by creating your dream,

you are pulling it towards yourself.

Be specific because grand sweeping ideas may arrive in ways you do not expect or with outcomes you do not anticipate.

Instead, live in it.

Let that be a happy place.

The more you visualize, the more you emotionalize, the easier

and faster it can arrive.
Opportunities will be presented.
Your actions will change.
New opportunities will be shown.

There is so much beauty inside each and every one of you.
There is so much possibility.
There is so much light.
You only need to break free from the box you have been put in.
Break free and find your joy.

THE FREQUENCY YOU EMIT

Phase one is creating the desire for Awakening.
Phase two is understanding your oneness, understanding your connection with everything that is around you – your connection with the Earth,
with the beings and the objects of the Earth –
and understanding how to work with your spirit, your soul, and your consciousness.
Understand how these elements work not only within you,
but also, how they work within the physical plane of the Earth,
with the energetic plane of multi-dimensions, the cosmos, the universe
and how to expand beyond yourself.
That is phase two.

First is to understand the universe.
The universe is multi-dimensional, multi-faceted, and has many planes.
You are in one reality.
Really, your mind is in one timeline.
You have the ability to switch between timelines, dimensions,

and between versions of you.

Decisions you made in alternate timelines may be different than the ones in this reality, so your life in different dimensions can be very different.

The decisions you make change your reality and change your dimension.

Understand that this is a bigger topic than this one message – a fundamental understanding of how much more you are – and it is important to be able to transcend who you are today.

To expand your mind past your physical being, you must understand how the world outside your physical being works.

The world is not linear.

Time is not linear.

Your understanding of reality is linear, so you must change your understanding of the way the world is designed.

You must understand there are dimensions, portals, wormholes, and wrinkles in time.

These things exist, but that is not what I'm talking about.

Today, it is about understanding your ability to manipulate time, space, matter, and reality.

The fundamental understanding will be Law of Attraction because that works within the constructs of the energetic word.

You are creating ties to objects you desire or to the actions you desire, so you pull them towards you.

When that happens, the energetic field radiates from you, pulses from you and pulses around the world. This energy does not stop once it is created.

Now picture you have radio waves (you can think of them in this way, it's not actually like that) but there are invisible waves coming from you. We all have transmitters and understand the waves even though you do not see them. If you desire an object to come into your life, what you are doing is sending out waves. The receiver (or the object) picks up your signal. Now there is a connection made between you and the object you desire. The more you think about this object, the more you feel it in your hands, the more real it comes, the closer it comes to you. This attraction could be based on the choices you are making – consciously or unconsciously – that are bringing you closer to the object, or the object's spirit feels your desire and creates or aligns circumstances for you to come into its life because it feels you drawing it near.

We have established that everything has a spirit, and everything has a consciousness. So, you are working with other consciousnesses to connect. In this connection, there are multiple things happening, but understanding the energy you create within yourself is the fundamental process.

This is the basis of everything you will do moving forward – understanding that the thoughts you have running through your brain every single second are creating your reality.

What did you think about today?
Did you think about hopeful things? Happy things? Sad things? Frightful things? Whatever it was, this is what you are pulling towards you.

We established that you are emitting energy waves.
This is your frequency that you are sending out.
There are messages coded within the frequency about what you desire, what you are pulling towards you, and what you are creating and energy waves with what you desire (good or bad) are speaking to the consciousness of what you want.

A connection is established, which creates an energetic line between you and the object. The stronger you desire it, the more time you think about this object, and the depth of emotion you feel about having this object in your possession in the moment affects when you receive it. Even if you do not possess it, you have to picture having it in the present. If you picture it in the future, it will stay in the future as this is where you are keeping it. You have to live in it now and you must feel it at this moment. The more you live in the moment with the object and how it makes you feel, the stronger and faster you will pull it towards you.

You are creating vibrational alignment.

Until vibrational alignment is created, you will not have the object.

I need to keep this simple because the more you try to overanalyze it and pick this apart, the farther the object is getting. You do not have to figure out the how, you only need to figure out the what.

What do you want?

What do you dream of?

What does your perfect life look like?

Your happy life, your fulfilling life?

Your life with unconditional love, beauty, and every desire you ever wanted, because you can live that life.

I say that you can live the life of your dreams, but please understand, the life you dreamt before you were spiritually awake may not be the same life you desire after you are spiritually awake. You will find that material objects and societal pressures that tell you what you should want do not mean as much.

So, understand the dream you make today may evolve, and that is okay. Keep pulling it towards you and be gentle with yourself as things change and evolve.

Create dream boards of the beautiful vision of the life you want to live – the life you desire – and put yourself there.

Live in your imagination and in your dreams,
and the more you can do this, the more you are creating opportunities for that life to come into play, into alignment.
Find the beauty. Find creativity and pull your dreams towards you.

BE PRESENT

I mentioned you are a multidimensional being.
I mentioned you will be able to jump between time and realities and speak telepathically.

There are many things that need to happen before this occurs before you understand your true ability. There are other teachers working on this specifically.
What you need to do is throw out many of the organized concepts you have of your reality.
Also, stop living by time.
Stop being obsessed with time and start living in the present.
By building constructs of time, your obsession with the past and future have become lopsided.
You are not living in the present.

The present is where you get to enjoy life.
This is where things are happening at this moment.
Are you enjoying it or are you thinking about the situation that happened yesterday that hurt you, or in the future thinking about what could go wrong?
Those thoughts are not serving you.
Although you need planning and forethought in your human life, the obsessive thought process, overanalyzing situations and conversations, reliving traumas of the past, and pondering what you could have done differently all need to be redirected to living

in the moment.

Find the beauty of this moment.

What is going right in your life?
What are you happy about?
What are you excited about?

When you go into the future, focus on what you want to bring into your life such as more happy and joyful times. When you go into the past, focus on what brought you joy and an experience you don't mind reliving.
You must learn to enjoy the present.

What are you doing at this very moment?

Feel this moment.
Stop and feel your breath.
Look around and find five beautiful things.
Five things that make you happy.

At this very moment, stop and breathe.

Start to make this a habit.
Start to make this part of your day: To stop and to be still.
Stop and watch this moment and appreciate it for what it is.

Understand that this moment will pass, but be present here at this very moment, this second, living, watching, and breathing.
Enjoy the people around you as a gift – as a gift of life, as a gift of being human.
The more you can live in this moment, the more you can be open and live beyond today, but it needs to start with today, this moment, this second: Stop and be.
Be here.
See the beautiful radiance of today.

EXPAND YOUR CONSCIOUSNESS BEYOND YOU

See your consciousness beyond your brain.
See your consciousness within every cell of your body.
See your consciousness moving out from your physical body, expanding into the space around you – expanding, becoming bigger than you.
Start by expanding a couple inches beyond your skin.

You will work your way out but stay small until you are ready to move farther.

When you start working with your consciousness and start expanding it, make sure to ask your spirit allies to protect you as you do this work. You have many protector beings in the Spirit World. Once you are Awakened, you will carry a natural protection with you. If you have not gone through the Awakening Activation yet, then I suggest completing prior to practicing expanding your consciousness. There is a protection that comes with it. If you want to do this work, but you do not have access to the guided activation or you are not ready to take that step, then ask your protector beings to protect you as you work to expand your consciousness.

I want you to close your eyes and see yourself as a ball of light.
You can be any color you want, or no color, clear, translucent or neon.

Your ball of light is contained within your physical being.
As you continue to practice, grow this light larger.
The light is attached to you, it is attached to your consciousness within your body.
See this light expand and contract with your breath.

Take a deep breath in... and let it out.

See the light contract and grow with your breath, much like your heartbeat.

It will keep with the rhythm of your breath.

It does not need to move a lot, it can slightly pulse.

It is alive. It is a part of you.

It is much like an organ within your body – your beating heart, your expanding lungs, your diaphragm moving up and down, and your muscles that contract and constrict.

Continue to watch your light contract and expand.

Watch the light in your mind. Close your eyes and visualize your consciousness moving beyond you. Keep it small in the beginning and continue to practice.

Watch your consciousness expand.

Eventually, bring your light a couple inches beyond your physical body.

Do not expand past that yet. We will get to that in later lessons.

Right now, it is about working with your own energy.

Understand this is your energy and your light.

This is your consciousness.

You are just learning how to feel it.

You are learning how to see this light be a part of you – how to feel it grow, and understand you have power over what it does.

You have control over how it works. Make sure to do this in an area where you feel safe and can truly relax.

You can also do this while lying in bed.

It is a great way to relax before going into the Dream World.

You may find you have extra vivid dreams because the connection between you and your consciousness is what will grow your dreams, what will grow the Dream World inside of you.

Hear the messages that come through the dreams in an objective way.

Do not take them literally.

When something happens in your dreams, ask yourself: How does it make me feel? How does it make me think or look at something or the situation? Do I feel like I need protection? Do I feel fearful? Could my dreams be showing me something that is going on? Could there be answers shown to me? Or is it just bringing an unconscious thought form into my conscious mind?

As you practice, relax.

Relax your mind.

If you meditate, think of this in a similar way.

If you do not meditate, possibly find teachings that are comfortable to you.

It is not required, but it can help quiet your mind.

It can help you understand the quietness within that is available to you.

It relaxes the body and fosters connection.

Allow yourself to breathe, reflect, and connect because this is truly about connection.

If you are looking for a connection within, there are wonderful teachings and guidance to support you.

Find something that feels right to you, even if it is only five minutes a day.

That five minutes can recharge and give you an insight into your soul that you would not have without those five minutes.

Find your time to connect.

Find your time to be present.

MULTIDIMENSIONAL BEING

Today, we are going to talk about the future – Your future, the Earth's future, and the future of mankind.

The future holds many things, many dimensions that are not yet created.

Dimensions are like a page in a book. They are connected, yet they stand alone.

The actions that are taking place right now on Earth are creating multiple realities.

This is happening through choice, vibration, thought, and the intention to create.

Possibly, you do not understand what you are doing with this work. You are creating a new reality, a new dimension with information and an outcome that transcends the possibilities of previous realities.

The actions in this reality will create a wormhole that contains all possibilities, creating distance between the negative energies contained on Earth and a safe place for Ascension to happen.

You asked to create this and now it is in play.

It is being created and the foundation is being laid. You are not the only person who is energetically creating this. There are others, and there are more to come.

I want you to take a moment to reflect.

To reflect on your life.

To reflect on your awakening.

To reflect on what is to come.

Right now, you are creating a new life, a new dream, and a new reality for yourself because you have chosen to make this change. You have chosen to make this leap of faith.

You have chosen to participate in this message, in its delivery, and in enlightenment.

The profound nature of the words flowing have not yet sunk in.
These words have not yet been realized by the world and have yet to be embraced by the heart.
As these changes take place within others, within those around you, within the world, within your community, things will begin to move more quickly.

Right now, this is about movement.

Movement in one direction, and there is a lot of groundwork that must take place before that movement is realized, actuated, and fulfilled.
Before there is a flame, there must be a spark.
What goes into making a spark and a sustaining flame? Many things.
Often, much work and preparation go into building the foundation, the lattice work, for the flame to take hold and create a sustaining fire.
See the work that you do now as creating the base and the framework for when the spark occurs. When the spark happens, it will ignite and take off.
This is much like the change that will happen in many people's lives.
This will happen in your life.
It will happen in your friend's lives and to your neighbors, to your community, to your country, and to the world.
This will spread like wildfire.

There is not a simple explanation that will help you understand dimensions.
Just know the choices you make define your direction for the multiple realities you live in.

Your consciousness lives a multi-dimensional life.

Your consciousness is split between multiple realities, multiple dimensions, multiple times, multiple versions of you, and multiple versions of humanity.

Your soul, and your consciousness, can be divided and yet be whole.

How can that be?

You think of yourself as a physical being who is self-contained, but that is not how it works.

Your consciousness is a multidimensional being.

You are made to live in multiple places at one time.

So, the concept of being self-contained in a human body needs to change.

You need to see yourself within a leaf on a tree, within a flower on the ground, within a rock under your feet, because you could be there.

You could be anywhere because your consciousness is greater than you.

Your consciousness is beyond you.

You are connected to every living and non-living being.

I will let that sink in for today.

I will let the concept of your individuality erode and break away.

Your understanding of your connectedness will grow.

Let your concept of individuality lessen.

It will always be there, and it is an important aspect of you, but as you move through these teachings, you will understand your connectedness to the world has a greater effect on you as an individual than you have any understanding or concept for.

Allow the belief within you to grow and expand your connectedness with the Earth, with the beings on Earth, with everything, and with the world around you.

It will not diminish your oneness; it will only create balance as currently your concept of individuality is far greater than your concept of connectedness. It is lopsided and must even out.

Allow your individuality to remain an aspect of you, but not the whole understanding and definition of you.

You are greater than this planet.
You are truly greater than this universe.
You see this universe as a singular object; however, it is not.
It is many, it is a multiverse.

See yourself connected, flowing, and rolling with the hills.
See yourself floating upon the wind.
See yourself as the rays of sunshine hitting leaves.
See yourself as the animals in the forest.
See yourself within other humans.
See yourself within your friends, your family, and those you do not know.
See yourself within those who are different from you and those you do not understand. You are connected, and you are one.
Love everyone for who they are and what they represent, even if it is not something you agree with.

Freedom of thought is a beautiful thing.
Freedom of opinion is a beautiful thing.
Freedom of individuality is a beautiful thing.
Being one – connected and intertwined – is a beautiful thing.
Live, love, and embrace all.
Find love within yourself, let it bloom, and your love for oneness will also bloom.

THE TIME OF ENLIGHTENMENT

Today, we are going to discuss the planets that are alive.

Life, as you know it, is a fragile thing.

Life requires a balance – a symbiosis, an interconnectedness within all life, within all beings, and within all objects.

Earth is not the only planet that sustains life.

There are many others.

They all hold different purposes, and they all offer experiences to souls.

Some planets serve the purpose of collectivity.

Some serve the purpose of higher cognitive thinking.

Some planets are like Earth and others are very different.

Other planets offer an experience, but they do not offer free will.

The mission, objective, or purpose of the soul's life is predetermined.

There is an ability to select a path and choose the method that moves you from A to B.

However, B is ultimately the goal and where one will end up.

Free will is the objective of Earth.

Free will and Enlightenment.

There are a few things to note:

Enlightenment is a beautiful spark within the soul – an ascension of vibrational levels.

Enlightenment was always the purpose and goal.

Enlightenment has become more difficult.

Enlightenment for all is no longer possible.

Enlightenment for few has taken place.

Enlightenment for many is upon the horizon.

Enlightenment is a process.

Enlightenment is a process that requires the will of the mind and soul to work together to achieve it.

Work is required to shed the confines of society's teachings.

Enlightenment will become the next new thing.

To become mainstream, enlightenment must reach thousands, if not millions, of people.

The time of Enlightenment is born.

The time of expansion of the mind has arrived.

The expansion of what is possible, what is accepted, and what is understood will change.

The confines of your science will change.

The lotus flower of consciousness will bloom.

The desire will grow inside many.

The time is upon you to look inside, to see your beautiful souls, and to see you are so much more.

The possibilities of this life are greater than what you ever imagined.

The time spent within your mind must be focused on what is to come in a beautiful way – to create the future, to create harmony, and to create the peace that is to come.

To create acceptance and love for all mankind and all living beings.

The time is now to let go of the limiting thoughts.

The time is now to let go of self-doubt and fear.

This path that you have chosen, this path of Enlightenment, can be beautiful and easy, but you must believe, and you must create it.

This path of Enlightenment is open to all.

All are welcome.

All are encouraged, but each person must choose it.

LEAP OF FAITH

The time is now to move forward with your dreams – your dreams of Enlightenment, your dreams of sharing, your dream of living the life you know is possible.
Now is the time to transform what is into what can be.

The life you are living is beautiful, precious, and all-encompassing. To create freedom, shifts need to happen within oneself – an opening, an allowing, and a leap of faith.

A leap of faith can mean many things.
A leap of faith can be within your mind or within the physical world.
A leap of faith is a commitment.
It is a powerful shifting of directions.
It is not to be irresponsible.

It is not to be misguided.
This is a calculated choice and commitment being made – a commitment to your future, a commitment to yourself, a commitment to change.

In many ways, it is severing your old ways and your old life.
It is fully immersing yourself in the new life.
By making a leap of faith, you are all in.
You are committed.

When you keep options and backup plans, there is a lack of commitment.
When there is a lack of commitment, there is also doubt and fear, and that is what we are trying to get you to move through.
Move through the doubt.
Move through the roadblocks you put before yourself energetically, consciously, or even unconsciously.

Recognize them as roadblocks.
Recognize them as they are created and placed in front of you.
Recognize where they came from.

Did you create this energetically with your thoughts?
Did those thoughts come from your conscious mind or your unconscious mind?
What mantra, affirmation or phrase can you use to rewrite that thought process?

Rewrite the thought process to be able to move forward.
You cannot take a leap of faith and continue to hold all the baggage from your current life.
You must shed the layers first.
You must work through the roadblocks before you,
and when you have reached the edge where the road has taken you, you will know.
You will know when it is time.
You will know when it is time to leap forward.

Make changes in your life.
Choose your happiness.
Choose the wonderful world that is placed before you with its infinite possibilities, infinite happiness, and infinite joy.
Feel all that is possible.
Know this is yours.
Know you only need to reach out and grasp it.

Change your thoughts and change your beliefs – beliefs of what can be and beliefs of the limiting world you live in.
Understand that there is so much more.
Understand that the possibilities are endless.
Understand that your human life has so much more potential.

Find your happiness, find your joy, and leap into your new life.

Part 3

EXPANSION OF YOU

CHAPTER 10: HOW DO I EXPAND INTO ALL THAT I AM THAT I CANNOT YET SEE?

The light from the stars touches your soul because you come from the stars.

EXPANSION OF FREQUENCY

Welcome, my dear Serraphine.

We begin this journey of understanding, of integration, of expansion, of the being who you truly are – as a person, as a spirit, and as a consciousness. The being that you are walks the physical earth, experiencing physical things, yet it is an illusion to who you truly are.

Who you truly are is an energetic being, living a human experience and a physical experience.

The experience of this human life is limited by the belief of who you are and what you can do.

As you walk forward in this understanding and teaching, you walk forward into the potential that you contain – the potential expansion of your mind, your physical form, your energy body, your abilities, understanding, and communication.

Dive deep into the understanding of who you are at the core.

Dive deep into who your soul is and why you have come.

For many, the human experience is about expanding your soul's capacity for frequency, your soul's capacity for experience, your soul's capacity for the endless possibilities that you are.

When you are born into the human world, you forget everything. You forget all your lives and all your past experiences, and you start anew.

You create a concept of self and worth by your family and culture, and you're taught belief systems.

What if all these teachings and experiences were wiped away, and you became a clean slate? Who could you be?

You would be many things, many beings, and many experiences. Your experience on planet Earth is not limited to the human mind.

Your soul experiences planet Earth as the animals, plants, rain drops, or leaves on a tree, and these experiences build your understanding of what life is. It builds your understanding of what your potential is and who you choose to be.

The consciousness that resides within a leaf retains the memories of all lives – of self, oneness, individuality, connection and flow, dependency, and independence.

This flow of information, tranquility, and experience builds the understanding of the planet and of what humans can be and understand.

The expansion of frequency in the human consciousness allows a greater breadth of experience.

By expanding the vibrational frequencies allowed to enter Earth, we expand the possibilities and experiences of humans.

Not all humans will choose to expand into these outer reaches of frequency, but those who do pave the way for others, and bring more technology, more information, and more growth.

To create a world of limitless possibilities and depth of understanding, you must expand.

To expand, you must turn within.
The expansion is not on the physical Earth, it is within your soul, consciousness, and understanding of who you are, who you are meant to be, and who you came here to be.
You were meant to be more.
You were always meant to be more and as you expand, you understand more.

Seek teachings that expand your mind and the frequencies you hold.
Always feel with your heart for the frequency of love. Love is the language of your soul.
Love is the language that will expand the mind.
Let love be your guide because that is who you are: You are love.

Contain, stream, and flow your love.
You are the frequency of love. Give it freely and watch it grow inside and out.

PROTECTIONS & VIBRATIONAL INTENTION

A Seraphim Angel, God, and I are sitting at a small round bistro table.

Thank you Serraphine and friends for being here. Today, we talk about protections that you have as humans walking the Earth. Protections sound like an odd topic to bring up, however, the way the energetic world works, you become vulnerable without protections.

We use the word protections, but I do not think of them that way

– they are more about intentions – intentions of what you allow and what you do not allow.

You choose the energies and frequencies that come in and out of your energetic field.
You do that through intention, choice, and thought.
You can also prevent energies from coming into your energetic field with intention, choice, and thought.
Without intention, choice, and thought regarding your energetic protections, you have none.

Understand that you need to ask to be protected. Why? And what does that look like?
This is an important step. It is simple, it is instant, and all you need to do is ask.
You all have guardian angels, guardian beings, and guardian allies.
Those allies must be invited to work with you, otherwise, they are not honoring your free will.
Divine beings always honor free will.

Your energetic friends, allies, and teachers want to work with you.
They want to be by your side and to be there for you, but you need to invite them to join you and walk the Earth with you. You need to invite them to protect your energies as you walk in a dense – and sometimes unruly – place.

As the Earth transitions and splits into the New and Old Earth, the dense energies will become more prolific and more abundant. This is because there are more high-vibration energies being requested by those seeking the New Earth. The New Earth is bringing a new high-vibrational frequency to the planet. When this happens, there must be an equal and opposite action because the current Earth requires balanced energies of light and dark.

To provide balance, denser, darker, and lower frequencies are also coming in.

This is what is creating the divide – it is pulling apart the poles of love and despair.

Those frequencies are becoming more intense and stronger.

As those frequencies become more intense, you must intend that only high frequencies are welcomed into your energetic field.

You get to say, you get to choose, and you get to choose with intention, choice, and thought.

If you intend to walk the Earth only feeling, experiencing, navigating high vibration, that is what you are welcoming.

This intention is an easier process than having no intention at all.

Intend you are safe.

Think and choose your safety, protection, and guidance, and it will be there every step of the way.

VIBRATIONAL ALIGNMENT

As you expand your energetic frequency and vibration, you not only expand your energetic being, but also the frequencies that you can hold and how much more light you can contain.

You all contain densities within you, as you live in a dense human world.

However, as you welcome more light, more high frequency/ vibration words, actions, and thoughts, these high-vibration actions, words, and thoughts change the frequency you emit.

As you raise your personal vibration, you then shift the balance of light and dark within you.

As you welcome more high frequency, you push out the denser frequencies you carry.

However, as you release and push out these denser energies you contain, it can often be uncomfortable.

You often must release, forgive, and change your thought process, your belief system, your belief in others, your acceptance of others, and the anger contained inside of you.
These dense frequencies no longer match the higher frequency of your human body, of your energetic body, and as you shift from them, you welcome in more light.

You must release the shadow and densities you carry.
To release shadow or densities, you may need help.
You may need help in recognizing the patterns you hold, the beliefs you have, and the thoughts running through your mind.
You will need to heal past traumas and forgive those who harmed you.

Choose to focus on happiness, gratitude, and love.
Choose to bring your loved ones and friends closer to you in love and friendship.
As you release, you make more room for greater happiness, joy, and abundance in your life.
By welcoming in higher frequencies, requesting them to come, intending them to come, choosing them to come, you increase your personal vibration.

Your personal vibration is an important piece in understanding your enlightenment.
Your personal vibration is a signal to the energetic world for what you desire and what you call towards you.

As you raise your personal vibration, you begin to change your life.
Your personal vibration is your calling card.
As you move higher and higher in vibrational planes, you begin to

change the way the world interacts with you.

As you release densities, as you request more high frequencies into your person energetic field, you begin to ascend vibrationally into new levels or vibrational dimensions.

As you cross thresholds into new vibrational dimensions, the activities and the hardships of the Earth change.

As you contain a higher personal vibration, you must resonate with the vibrational dimension you reside in.

As you gain higher frequencies in your personal energetic field, you change what is available to you.

As you ascend, you will move through vibrational ceilings, removing possible experiences from your world and dimension.

Of course, you can always choose to change, invite in, or welcome back the densities you have released.

You can always go back down or come back up.

This is your free will.

As you ascend vibrational dimensions, you will have other options presented to you.

Other options that create change, not only inside of you and your vibrational field, but also inside the world around you.

Sometimes, the change you are requesting in the physical world can only be created by aligning, changing, upgrading, or downgrading your personal vibration.

Your personal vibration calls out to experiences around you – it seeks actions and relationships with the same frequency.

By understanding the importance, the relationship, and the cause and effect of personal vibration, you begin to understand your personal responsibility for yourself, your choices, your thoughts, your actions, and the experiences you are exposed to and welcome into your life.

This comes not through choice and thought, but by frequency and unconscious thoughts.

Understanding your personal frequency has a great effect on your life.
Learn more about your personal frequency.
Learn how to understand it, how to change it, and how to intend where you want it to be.

You live in an energetic world, and you are an energetic being,
but you do not understand how your energetic choices affect you.
Seek this information.
Seek these teachings.
This is how you grow; this is how you will change.

Feel and understand where you want to be and where you want to go.
The New Earth welcomes you.
We invite you.
You get here by changing your vibrational alignment, your frequency to align with the New Earth.
Call the New Earth and she will come.

She will help you release the densities that you carry.
She will help you, and she will protect you.
Call her and desire her.
You have so much help, and there are many teachings to support you.
Your vibrational frequency is the key to the New Earth.

THE NEW EARTH

The New Earth – what is this place we discuss?
What is the evolution of the human consciousness?

The New Earth is the enlightenment of humans who choose to ascend to the full potential of their unconscious mind.
The New Earth is a collective civilization of humans who choose a vibrational frequency to live in peace, harmony, and within the frequency of love.

Since the Earth has the purpose of free will, those who do not choose to ascend to the New Earth will stay in the Old Earth.
Free will must be honored, so both options are being created.
Those who choose to move to the New Earth vibrationally and energetically will eventually physically move to this location after all current humans have chosen.
The divide will be chaotic as people choose as you are mixed in the Old and New Earth.

Currently, you are like oil and water shaken up, still moving to the poles of love and despair.
Over time, it will become easier.
Over time, it will become clearer.
Over time, it will move into a graceful flow.
Until we reach that point, there must be time to provide teachings to all humans so they can have an informed choice.
They have an understanding, and they can reconnect.

Enlightenment of humans was a primary purpose of the Earth; however, things got a little off track along the way, which brings us to this time of awakening.
Actually, it is truly a time of re-Awakening.
Everyone holds within them the keys to awakening, to ascension, and to enlightenment.

You discover the keys by reconnecting all parts of your soul and consciousness to Source within the infinite universe, Source within the planet, and Source within yourself.

You are in a web of energetic connections.
Energetic connections race through the human body.
Yet, the conscious mind does not recognize them.

Yet, you are hard wired to feel, and understand the energies happening around you.

The New Earth is a harmonious collective of people who live together in peace –
an ebb and flow of respect, of evolution, of technologies that will help to restore the planet.
A healthy symbiosis between the planet, animals, and people.
A collective intention of harmony, respect, and love.

The New Earth is humans' evolution and the next step for their development – a next step of their expanded mind and abilities.

To expand one's abilities is to expand into the energies, information, and frequencies around them.
It is to understand how the Earth, the Universe, matter, physics, quantum physics, the mind, thoughts, energies, and vibrations actually work.

Allow your mind to reach beyond your physical form.
Allow your energetic field to feel and relate to the world around you.
Allow your soul to erupt from inside of you to begin guiding you in your life's purpose and course.
Allow your soul to speak your truth.
Allow your soul to guide you, to comfort you, to educate you, and move into who you truly are – who you truly want to be and who you desire to be.
In love, in happiness, in a life of joy.

The life you currently live is a facade for what is actually happening.

Peek behind the curtain to understand the full human potential and the energetic capabilities of your mind, of your soul, and of this planet to have a better understanding of who you are and what you desire.

Every person is different and has varying desires. By tapping into your soul and letting it shine, you not only expand the understanding of you, but you also create a connection with everything, with Source, within yourself, within the planet, and the universe, and you let your light shine. All of you.

Find your light. Find your authentic you. Step into the next phase of you.

EVOLUTION OF HUMANS

We are at the turning point for humans on planet Earth.
Many will evolve into the New Earth – into the next phase of human evolution, of human enlightenment, and human ascension.
And many will choose not to change.

For those who choose not to come, we honor their free will.
We honor their decisions and choices because we honor them as a person.
We honor what they believe is right, and we honor what they choose.
No one can do the work for them.

Even holding someone's hand will not bring them to the New Earth.
They must choose for themselves.
They must choose within their heart.
They must do the work to shed the densities and the programming

that society has given them.

You can only save yourself.
You can only choose for yourself.
Every person must choose for herself or himself.
This is not an outwardly decision.
This is not an outwardly path.
This is a path within one's soul, within one's mind, and within one's physical form.

Allow those seeking to test the waters to understand by providing information and guidance, but at the end of the day, they must choose.
To ascend to the New Earth, one must cross a vibrational plane, a vibrational dimension.
This vibrational dimension of the New Earth creates a divide, a separation between the densities of the Old and New Earth. Densities of the Old Earth do not influence those people who have vibrationally crossed the plane into the New Earth in the same way.

Everyone has access to this.
Every person walking the planet is born with the ability of ascending to the New Earth. Everyone has access.
Everyone must choose and learn.

Some cultures will have more access than others.
Some people will have more densities to shed to reach the New Earth vibrational plane.
But it does not mean they cannot make it.
And it does not mean it is a quick trip.

There are many people walking the Earth today who are Master Teachers – Ascended, Enlightened Master Teachers who are here to guide people to the New Earth.

There are many paths to the New Earth. There are many teachers leading the way.

Understanding vibrational frequency, the power of thought, the power of the mind, intention, and vibrational frequency will help guide you.

Emotional health and emotional restitution must be accomplished as the insecurities and trauma of your world do not exist in the New Earth.

To reach the vibrational frequency needed for the New Earth, every person must heal their emotional body, their mind, their unconscious mind, and their limiting beliefs.

There are many avenues to heal these mental and emotional wounds and every person must find their own path in doing this.

People must also change their perception of who they are.

The New Earth does not contain a population of individuals, rather it contains a collective of beings who fight for the greater good for each other, their society, and their planet.

They see themselves as a symbiotic, seamless part of a community, not an individual fighting for their own betterment.

That vibrational frequency does not exist in the New Earth.

Those entering the New Earth will still evolve.

With the creation of the New Earth, there are new frequencies requested on Earth.

Those higher frequencies are only available within the New Earth, so people will continue to evolve.

With the higher frequencies and higher dimensions come greater human abilities, technologies, and an expanse into the universe, the solar system, and an understanding of communication, participation, and integration with Intergalactics.

With the request of higher frequencies on the New Earth, there is also a request for denser frequencies on the Old Earth, plummeting them farther into denser frequencies of despair and fear.

We are at a turning point where both love and fear are prevalent, are intertwined, and are pervasive. You must seek out what you desire in this life and if that is love, if that is expansion, find the higher frequencies, the teachers, the information, knowledge, wisdom, and abilities that will support you.

Understand you are meant to be more, more than this human life. The New Earth allows evolution to take place, but it must be chosen, it must be understood, and reconnection must occur – reconnection of your soul to the Earth and to the Universal Consciousness, to teachings, and the shedding of densities.
Find your path, find your teachings, and find the joy within.
Find the love that radiates within you, from within your soul.
Connect, ask, and do the work.

EXPANSION OF THE MIND

Expansion of the mind is more than your unconscious connection with the collective consciousness, Source energy, or connection with self. The expanded mind understands how to influence time, matter, space, dimensions, and realities.

You are a multidimensional being, which I have said many times; however, you do not understand what a multidimensional being is yet.
You are not taught, nor do you have a great understanding of the complexities of the human soul.

The human soul exists in many places, times, dimensions, realities, and universes all at the same time. The human soul exists everywhere, all at once, at the same present moment.

How can that be, you asked?

It can be because you do not have a conceptual understanding of how your soul works – how time and space works, how dimensions work, and how the universe operates.

You live in this moment in your present mind.

Your present mind is in infinite locations at this present moment. You have the ability to jump between your own mind in different timelines, within different realities, different dimensions, and different universes.

How, you asked? How do you access these other versions of you? There are many teachings, some safe and some unsafe, to move within the human consciousness.

I share this with you today, not to share how, but to create the curiosity of what is to come.

This will be commonplace in the future of the New Earth in the not-so-distant future.

This is not a technology that is created.

This is an ability within your human mind that you currently hold.

It is understanding the parameters and safety measures, and it is understanding your own potential. This is moving into understanding how your human mind is created and wired.

To give a brief example on timelines:

There are infinite timelines on Earth. Timelines are created when decisions are made, and most humans have made many decisions in their lifetime. For example, a family decided to move across the country to take a different job that affected people in the household. The choice to take or not take a job changes each individual's life and creates a new timeline for all. Possibly, there is a version of the family that did AND did not take the new job.

It is possible to move between timelines, if they are close enough in action and in perception; however, once a timeline for an individual reaches a point you cannot switch between timelines because of significant differences. At this point, dimensions are created.

Dimensions contain multiple timelines.
Timelines branch off into other dimensions when timelines can no longer be switched between because the changes are too great.
Portals can be created between dimensions; however, they must be in close relation to one another.
Humans travel between timelines and dimensions quite regularly; you just do not realize it.

Each moment in time is not the way you perceive it.
A moment is like a page in a book. When your mind feathers the pages, you see a continuous story. However, each page stands alone and has other connecting pages – has other actions that happened – that changed the outcome and the future.
You can split one moment in time multiple ways, not just one or two. There could be five outcomes with five timelines from one moment in time. There are infinite possibilities and infinite ways these timelines flow together.

By understanding your choices, your influence, and your perception, you change how you work within the timeline structure.
Some of this you can control while other things you cannot, but even understanding that you have a multidimensional model of time changes your understanding of your future, your purpose, and how you navigate this Earth.

We are in a time of division.
We are in a time of choice and consequence.
Understand that your choices have consequences within your life, within the timelines you reside, and the dimensions you are

contained within.

I will let this sit for now, but know your multidimensional nature is an important part of being a successful person, participant, and resident of the New Earth.

STRUCTURES WITHIN

How is the human body constructed?
How is the human body meant to relate to others – other humans, animals, the planet, and the universe?

Humans are structured to live successfully on Earth within their physical nature, their emotional nature, and their energetic nature. However, humans are currently out of sync in multiple ways. Because of the way humans are structured and designed, being out of sync has created imbalances within the human psyche, within the energetic and spiritual world, and within the planet herself.

How do you realign the structures of the human mind, human body, and the human collective?
It is about evolution. Evolution that is intended to be.
Those who choose to evolve with enlightenment, ascension and embracing their own awakening process, move into restructuring their human body.

This is not something that will happen immediately.

This is not something that will happen within many humans' lifetimes; however, as more connections, reconnections, and harmonies within the structures of the human body and energetic body move into place, more harmony will come to the physical form.

We are disconnected from the planet that we were intended to share a frequency with.

We are disconnected from Source energy, information, and technologies that are available to us through light, frequency, and desire.

As you move into harmony within yourself – and move into enlightenment and expand frequencies within the mind, body, and spirit – a reconnection is allowed to transform your physical form to create harmony and health.

Without harmony within all aspects of the human physical form, there is dis-ease, there is dis-harmony, and there is dis-connection.

Align your physical form, your energetic form, your mental form to create healing within the structures of your body. You are more than nerves and cells: You are energy, you are consciousness, and you are meant to be plugged into the system of the planet and the human collective consciousness.

You are meant to be plugged into the spiritual and energetic world to communicate, heal, and to request information.

Without these connections, you miss part of who you are as a human, part of the system you are intended to live within.

Find how to reconnect.

How to live within the energetic and spiritual world.

To connect, to flow, to find the peace and harmony that flows through you, from within you, and from within the planet and the cosmos.

Radiate love from within, reconnect to it, and let it transform the physical structures of your human physical form.

THE EARTH

I join a turtle sitting at the bistro table in God's House. I have a knowingness the turtle is representing the animals of the Earth in our coming discussion. We hold hands before God begins to speak.

Today, we will discuss the Earth.

The New Earth, the Old Earth, and the evolution of Earth.

The evolution of the Earth is tied to the evolution of the human species.

This happened and was planned with the creation of the planet.

Your destinies are linked through purpose, surrender, and choice.

Your planet Earth has a soul, and she has decided to evolve with humans.

To evolve with humans means that there must become two planets for both versions of humans to live – the humans who decide to evolve and move to the new Earth, and those who choose not to.

The Earth seems to be in turmoil, but she is truly in change.

She is changing her own identity and purpose. At this moment, there are two planets, the Old and New, living concurrently together and unfortunately, this creates chaos.

It creates chaos that you can see, feel, and know.

This evolving into a higher life form and de-evolving is taking place at the same time.

These changes are not only energetic, but they are also physical – much like the changes that are happening within each human who decides to evolve.

The changes are not only energetic, but they are also physical.

Physical changes start to take place once the choice of enlightenment and awakening has been made.

New energies flow to the body – the energy and frequency

149

of connection with Source, with universal love, light, and information. When this light is reconnected to the soul, physical changes start to happen – first, on a quantum level within the body, then atomic, then cellular, and then global.

These changes bring about many things: Greater awareness, perception of abilities, ability to energetically connect with the beings, animals, and objects around you.

These changes push out the shadow, the hurt, and the trauma of a human life to bring about healing.

To bring about the awareness of who you are, your place on the planet, and your relationship with others.

You also have access to healings that you did not have prior access to.

The frequencies of the universal light hold the ability to heal energetically, vibrationally, and physically. The desire to heal and change are important factors in this change, in this movement forward, and in this evolution. Much like the changes happening on the physical Earth, they mirror the changes happening inside the human body.

There is an evolution of cells, evolution of knowledge, learning, and peace.

Currently, our Earth is letting go, healing, and releasing denser parts of herself to evolve into an enlightened form.

This evolved Earth is where the evolved humans will co-exist and work together, live in harmony, symbiosis, and partnership.

The parts of the Earth that cannot be healed will fall away.

Old Earth's evolution will be different. Her progress, her knowledge, and her relationship with humans will be different.

The Old Earth serves an important purpose and thus the relationships between humans and the planet will be very different.

Both evolve together.

Learn to move within yourself to connect your energies with the New Earth and learn to work together with your enlightenment, awakening, and evolution. By connecting, grounding, and intending the connection, not only to Source energy, but with that of the New Earth, this will help create harmony within you. Allow these energies to flow, grow, and evolve.
Allow your connection with the New Earth to help you heal, move through your own transition, your own evolution, and your own awakening.

The New Earth is here to assist you, she calls to you.
Heed the call and connect.
Allow your senses to grow.
Allow your connections to grow.
Feel them within your soul, within your mind, and heart.
Connect, allow, and be.

Be present with the changes that are happening within you.
Be present with the changes that are happening within the Earth.
Live within your connections.
Be who you were always meant to be, much like the Earth who is evolving into who she was always meant to be.
You are on this path together.
Connect, join, and be reborn.

THE BEINGS AROUND

* My vision returns to God's House and the bistro table with the turtle. We release our hands, and the turtle gets down from the table. I feel he was representing the New Earth in the prior conversation. A new being enters the room and sits at the table. They feel like a troll, however, I have a hard time forming a clear image, but I can see they have blue hair.

You are surrounded by beings unseen.
Beings that are unseen by your naked eye.
Your eyes are not your only way to see.
You also see with your heart.
You see with every cell of your body.
Seeing with your eyes is a misconception – a misconception of the world that surrounds you.

What you see is true – there are cars, trees, and other physical beings, entities, and objects, but what you do not see are the frequencies of light that carry other souls.
Some of those souls you have named ghosts, while some are guardian angels, or animal spirit allies. However, there are more.
There are caretakers of the Earth that you do not see.

Your old wisdoms have referred to them in many ways. The fairies, trolls, sprites, and mermaids are also an important part of the Earth.
These are the caretakers of the Earth.
You do not see everything around you.
You do not understand the inner workings of the Earth, the forests, the animals, and the creatures.

Understand your part within this network of not only humans on the planet, but every creature, and soul that resides on planet Earth.
Some of these beings exist in your dimension while some exist in others, popping and flitting into yours to do the work, to care, and tend and to grow and expand.

Each being holds a different purpose within each community and within the Earth as a whole. These caretakers and tenders are an important part of the Earth's ecosystems, and yet, you have no connection to them, no understanding of them because you cannot scientifically test for them.

Learn to expand your awareness of other souls.
You cannot see them with your eyes, you can only feel them when you connect your souls.
You connect with them by expanding your awareness as you move through the planet's ecosystems, forests, and water lands.
There is more to this Earth than you understand.
There is more to your abilities than you understand.

By expanding your abilities, your gifts, and your skills only then can you expand into the understanding of this Earth. Only then will you understand how important she is to every being, creature, and human.
By allowing yourself to learn how to expand your knowingness, your sight, your hearing, and your connection, then you can connect into the vast expanse of possibilities that are around you.

Let this expansiveness be who you are.
Allow this channel, this awareness, this deep reserve of knowingness to find your voice and find your sight – to find all the pieces of you: Your abilities, your kindness, your love, and your connection within this beautiful Earth that you reside.

Part 4

AWAKEN

CHAPTER 11: ROADMAP TO AWAKENING

You were always meant to be great.
Allow yourself to believe it.

SPIRITUALLY AWAKE:

Awareness of the connection your soul has to the greater Energetic World and Source. A knowingness or audio connection with spiritual or energetic guides and teachers. The belief there is more and a desire to learn more.

AWAKENING PROCESS:

The process of fully connecting and integrating your soul with your conscious mind.

Establishing communication, understanding, and frequency connections between your soul and consciousness with your conscious mind to move into a more enlightened and connected state.

PRACTICAL ROADMAP

The human experience is complex, undefined, and can be overwhelming at times. We are at a time of enlightenment and transition into the next phase of the development of the human consciousness. Frequencies of change are flooding the Earth with new technologies, information, and possibilities. Not only is life on Earth complicated, but where you are headed is even more complicated.

Let Part 4 of this book be a basic framework that shows you how to move from where you are now to where you want to be. Each of these topics is a full course or book, so this is only a small overview. You will need to seek out teachings to fully develop these skills.

Find teachings with your heart and not your mind. There is no right way to your awakening and enlightenment. Search for teachings that lift you up and empower you to find your voice and individual process. You cannot follow in anyone else's footsteps. You must create your own path. These small teachings are meant to point you in the right direction so you can expand them on your own.

The light burning bright within you will guide your way. Let your light shine to free your soul and your passion for this human life.

Expand into all that you are and all that you are capable of being.

PYRAMID OF ASCENSION

The pyramid of ascension shows the progression to move through densities of this Earthly plane, and to move into a higher personal vibration.

Your personal vibration determines your life and determines your earthly experience.

To move into a happier, more joyful life, you must shed the densities you carry.

Love
Oneness
Grounding
Surrender
Rebirth
Manifestation
Release, Heal

Let the pain, the trauma, and the emotional wounds be healed to allow room for enlightenment.

Enlightenment is a term being thrown around and is becoming misunderstood.
Enlightenment is a process of becoming whole – wholly you in accessing and integrating you. All of you.
Your culture does not recognize the importance of the soul-consciousness- body- mind connection.
Instead, you put value on external rewards, rather than internal.
That is completely understandable, because you were not taught, and you are unaware.

How do you move from being unaware to connected?
How do you turn on a lamp if there is no light bulb?
You must take actions and steps to fix the situation.
You must learn, ask questions, and act.
Willing the light to turn on and visualizing it as on is a good practice and will call the experience towards you, but at the end of the day, you must take actions that will move you towards your goal.

If your goal is the light of enlightenment, where do you find this light bulb?

Know that it has always been inside you.
You just need to believe, know it is there, and reconnect to it.
Most people do not have the tools for this approach, so they must be taught. Do not fret, you still have it inside you, and it is easier to locate the connection than to create it from scratch.

Learn from teachers who have traveled to Earth with the purpose of re-connection.
Teachers come in all shapes, sizes, colors, types, models, and beliefs.

Why? So, you can find the right teacher for you.

No two people are the same, so there must be options because we honor free will.

When seeking teachings, feel with your heart.

Feel the information, frequency, and message with your heart.

Does this resonate? Does this lift me up? Does this feel true in my bones?

There is no one way to Enlightenment and many teachers are guiding people to the New Earth. These teachers create new teachers who take the baton to guide the next group of seekers.

The messages brought by different teachers may sound, look, and feel different, but the purpose may be the same: Ascension.

Ascension of the mind, body, consciousness, and soul.

How does your soul Ascend?

Ascension of your soul is a process by which you hold more light.

What is light?

Light is information, frequency, color, and vibration.

Light is the conduit of life here on Earth.

Without light from the sun, there would be no life.

Much like water – without water, life would not exist in the way we understand it.

Light and water are the building blocks of your human world.

What if I told you that your understanding of your human life is not correct?

What if I told you, you are walking the yellow brick road and there is another scene (or understanding) behind the curtain?

I want to pull back the curtain to show you how to start living your own version of a human life, with all the information available to you. You will always have free will to decide how, when, or why you use it. However, living without all the information has clouded your understanding of who you are, your relationship with those around you, and the understanding of how the world works.

Let's open your eyes in the dark so you can turn on your own light.
Let me show you how to connect to an infinite source of information, joy, and abundance.
You no longer need to live a life of scarcity and fear.
Learn how to become connected within you but also with the oneness that surrounds you. With assistance and growth, you can reach your full potential.

Live a life of excitement and joy because that is what you have intentionally chosen.

Be you. Be whole. Be in joy. Be in love.

ASCENSION ACTIVATIONS

The Ascension Pyramid shows the steps to move through your human densities to ascend into the vibrational frequencies of the New Earth. Follow these simple activations to learn how to release your energetic densities and to call in the frequencies of the New Earth, which is love.

I ask that you complete the Awakening Activation prior to any of the Ascension Activations. There is a level of protection and purpose when done in order. We shed the base layer densities to make room for expansion, growth, and love. For many, this will be difficult and for others this will be as natural as breathing.

Please understand, you are inviting your soul's presence into your daily conscious life to experience a purpose-filled and

divinely guided life of freedom. This is what you are asking.

The steps laid before you are meant to be a simple, yet profound road map to activate the Awakening Process within you. This will give you tools and skills to navigate your awakening process and ascension to enlightenment. This does not need to be complicated or hard; however, it does take commitment and purposeful actions.

Allow your heart to open as you follow these simple activations to strengthen your divine connection and awaken your soul's voice.

These activations are meant to be experienced in a meditative state. Read the description then close your eyes to create the experience and activation while meditating.

*RELEASE ACTIVATION

Take a moment to get comfortable. Possibly light a candle, turn on soothing music or put in ear plugs and find an eye cover (a scarf or sock will work). Intend for your divine and enlightened protector beings to surround you as you move into this activation. Know that you are safe and only that which brings you to the New Earth can happen to you.

Breathe deeply through your nose and release the breath slowly. Do this as many times as you need to get into a deeply relaxed state.

Imagine you are walking in an old growth forest. There are dense, wide trees around you, many dripping with moss. The path you walk is clearly defined even with the layers of leaves and twigs covering the ground. You hear the crunch of the leaves and snap of twigs with each step. There is a rhythmic sound while walking. You can smell the fresh rain still clinging to the soil and hear the rustle of the leaves as a light breeze picks up.

The path takes you to a small clearing with a shallow stream. There is a perfect sitting rock perched on the side of the stream, so you sit comfortably and remove your shoes. You slip your feet into the cold water and feel the cool rush of water over your toes.

You can feel the warmth of sunlight on your face as a bright ray of light surrounds you in a golden warmth. This light feels comforting, protecting, and nourishing, so you lean into this feeling.

You feel the urge to release the densities and shadow within your body that you are ready to let go. You desire to release all the hurt, pain, and trauma from this human life into the cold water. You feel the release start slowly and grow into a larger flow, releasing negative thoughts, emotions, hurt and anger, allowing it to flow into the water to be taken away.

You say, **"I choose to release all densities that no longer serve me. I release any and all energies that do not bring me to the New Earth."**

You continue to release and let go. Some of you may need to consciously choose to let go as emotions, situations, and thoughts surface in your mind. Choose to let them go.

Continue until you feel complete. Breathe, release and let go, forgive, accept and allow gratitude for all you have learned and experienced.

You can feel the denser, energies drain from your physical form, making room for something new. As you release, you also fill with the warm sunlight shining upon you. As you let go, you feel your head, neck and shoulders fill with warm light. The expansion of light continues as you release more and more. You continue to release and fill with light until your entire body glows. This sunlight is the light of divine love, hope, connection, oneness, and Source.

When you feel ready, you leave the stream and walk back to the forest path, knowing you can come back at any time to let go of anything that does not move you into greater joy, happiness, and peace within.

Take some time to sit quietly and notice the subtle changes taking place.

MANIFESTATION

Manifestation is the three-dimensional creation of your thoughts. Manifestation is harnessing the power of thought, desires, dreams, and creation to pull your desired life and objects towards you.

Manifestation is an important tool in your human life and the principles of the Earth.
To create, you must ask, desire, and allow.
To manifest, you must ask, desire, and allow.

Allow the flow of your heart's desires to pull forth items, situations, and knowledge into this three-dimensional world. You do not yet know the power and abilities you have. Learn to harness manifestation and you will expand your understanding of the world and your potential.

This segment is not meant to teach you full manifestation, but only a snippet. Seek out expanded teachings to fully develop your ability to manifest.

Dream of the life you desire to start the creation process. There is no right way to do this, it is only right for you. Find teachings that align with these principles to become an expanded version of you and to draw forth the life of your dreams.

We are love at our core.

The frequency of love: God, Creator, self-love, connection with self and something greater are all connected with love.

How do you find this connection?
Step into the light of love and dance with your own shadow.
Recognize your fears, beliefs, and thoughts that hold you back from manifesting what you want in your life.
By releasing and creating space for new things, you then shift your life in a new direction.
As you peel away the layers of shadow and densities, you will start to reveal your true desires.

We are going to move through a couple of exercises to shake up your shadow and light balance. Most people in your modern world carry many densities, ego-based belief systems, and self-deprecating thoughts, as you were not taught differently.
How do you release something you do not know is there? Why do some things affect you in certain ways? Why do you have irrational thoughts or beliefs?

Let's start with the basic law of attraction: Like attracts like.
Like frequencies attract and pull the same frequency toward one another.
The frequency of your thoughts, emotions, and actions creates more of the same into the future – more of the same thoughts, emotions, and actions.

This is why thoughts are important in understanding the unconscious mind:
Desires create thoughts.
Thoughts create emotion.
Emotion creates frequency.

Frequency is what vibrates from you into the physical world.

The frequency you emit attracts the same frequency within situations, interactions with others, within opportunities, relationships, or objects.

I want you to take a moment to think about:

What is your frequency?

What is your primary emotion throughout the day? Is it stress, frustration, and conflict, or is it relaxation, joy, and love?

Whatever the emotion is, you are calling that frequency towards you.

How do you change your frequency?

Change your emotions and thoughts.

If you cannot change a situation, you can change how you feel about a situation.

Many times, you need to change your thoughts first before you can change your emotions.

Next level: Roadblocks

Roadblocks are thought patterns and belief systems that prevent you from manifesting.

These could be beliefs of not being worthy, being undeserving, not good enough, scarcity (lack of time / money), or powerlessness.

How do you move through these roadblocks?

How do you change a belief?

To manifest, you must heal the roadblocks within your mind that are keeping you from manifesting your desires.

Manifestation is also about moving into the flow of your life, the flow of your dreams, and the energetic river you are creating around you.

How do you move into a place of peace, grace, and ease?

First, you must create that state within your mind. Start by releasing densities, hurt, and pain in our activations to free the body of the energy blocks to make room for all the wonderful manifestations being created.

See how your thoughts and beliefs play a part in your life and creation of experiences.
See the energetic work you do in this simple construct: Give/release shadow, receive love and be in gratitude.

As you move through these exercises, see the work you do in this simple way:

Give, receive, be.

This will be a repeated process.

Give/Release Shadow

1. Recognizing and retraining thought patterns (energy healing, emotional support, and outside resources)
2. Healing trauma (this life and past lives). Again, you do not need to do this on your own. Seek emotional support and therapy to move through trauma and healing.
3. Reconditioning the mind (conscious & unconscious)
    *   Have your mind be a positive place full of gratitude and positive self-talk.
    *   Affirmations. Find affirmations that lift you up and speak to your soul.
    *   Change your belief systems by redirecting your thoughts so that they reflect how you want to view the world.

Receive Love

4. Believe you deserve the full spectrum of happiness in this human life.
    *   Receive help from others. Receive love from others.

- Grow your self-love.
- Let there be a balance of give and take between loved ones and relationships.

Be in Gratitude

5.   Move into the heart space of love and gratitude.

I invite you to write out your desires as it helps to create a clearer picture and stronger emotions when manifesting. Complete this exercise before doing the manifestation activation as it will strengthen your visualization, understanding, and creation.

Manifestation writing exercise

1.   Define your success or what you desire.
2.   What does your success or desired object FEEL like?
3.   Visualize your success, living in what you desire, creating a visceral experience.
4.   Release roadblocks. When a limiting emotion joins you, witness it, feel into it, accept it, heal it, and then move into gratitude.
5.   Let go, trust, and surrender.
    - Allow actions to flow through you to bring in what you desire.

As you experience struggle, difficult moments or hardship, see them as roadblocks and densities you still carry within you. Allow the difficult moments to be seen as teaching moments and a choice to release more. No one is testing you. We are showing you how to heal and what you need to choose to release. Continue to release to move through the layers of densities you carry.

*MANIFESTATION ACTIVATION

Take a moment to picture the life of your dreams – A happy, fulfilled life of self-love. What does it feel like, not the material objects, but the emotions of this life?
Possibly, you are:

- Surrounded by love - romantic, familial, and self-love.
- Free from expectations – cultural, family, religious or personal.
- Living a purpose-filled life.
- Financially free and living in abundance.

What does this version of you, who has everything you desire, feel like? Look like? How do they hold themself? How do they talk, walk, and act? Picture this person and his/her life clearly in your mind.

As you release and grow, this version of your ideal life will probably change, which is expected. Let this be a fluid dream and aspiration. Nothing is set in stone. As you change, your dreams change.

Take a moment to visualize your ideal life prior to entering the meditation.

Take a moment to get comfortable. Possibly light a candle, put on soothing music or ear plugs, and find an eye cover. Intend for your divine and enlightened protector beings to surround you as you move into this activation. Know that you are safe and only that which brings you to the New Earth can happen to you.

Breathe deeply through your nose and release the breath slowly. Do this as many times as you need to get into a deeply relaxed state.

Imagine you are in a forest surrounded by a dense grove of trees. You can smell the soft earth under your feet and hear birds chirping in the distance. There is a rustle in the bushes as small creatures move around in their homes. There is a light breeze that brushes your skin.

You see a grassy patch not far from the trail. There is a bright stream of light piercing the canopy above to show a clear ray of light. You know this light. You feel the connection with your divine self, with Source and divine love. It's like an old friend calling you home.

As you approach the grassy clearing, you see a person standing nearby. It is the version of you that has manifested your dreams. They have your future life, your desired life, and hold all the keys to being able to unlock the life you desire.

They greet you as you approach and you embrace in a warm hug, like old friends. You both walk into the ray of light together.

Within the bright light, you feel an exchange begin, where you call forth the frequencies of wisdom, healing, and purpose from the future you. They willingly share their gifts of knowledge, healing, and self-love with you. You feel their unconditional love for you and an excitement for you to create this dream life.

You feel wisps of energy, like a light breeze of light and frequency, dance and swirl around you. You feel the new frequencies of energy move into your physical body, into your cells, chakras, and energy systems, bathing you in a new light of possibility.

Once you feel the exchange is complete, thank your future self for sharing their fulfilled dreams. You walk out of the stream of light together and say a warm goodbye at the edge of the grassy clearing. You head back to the path where you started and back to your physical body and mind.

Take some time to sit quietly and notice the subtle changes taking place.

REBIRTH & DEATH

You have accepted the cycle of life as birth, growth, reflection, and death.

This is much like the cycle of seasons – Spring, Summer, Fall and Winter.

There is also a cycle of emotions, beliefs, and actions that follow the same pattern.

You may create a belief or dream when you are a child and as you age, this belief may no longer serve you.

You are ever evolving.

To evolve, you must make room for new aspects of your life. To do that, you must allow things to die.

Death has been made to be a scary, unknown thing by many cultures and belief systems.

Yet, it is as natural as a baby being born – it is 100 percent a miracle, and no less important in the cycle of life. By consuming yourself in the fear of death, you are warping the natural cycle and flow. (Not purposely of course, but your unconscious natural fear distorts the process.) By understanding death's natural progression in life, you honor the stages of life and walk welcomingly into your rebirth.

In this conversation, we will discuss the death and rebirth of feelings, beliefs, and actions.

In the cosmos, it is your soul and consciousness that experiences rebirth. These entities can never die, they can only be transformed through the process of rebirth.

Rebirth is the moment after death when space has been created.

It is a void of nothingness that is created for change and growth to be born.

A void of nothing can sound scary, but that is the moment of all potential.

Rebirth is a moment of infinite possibilities of creation.

When in your life have you felt like you had infinite possibilities of creation?
The purpose of this rebirth is to create room for what you desire.
Rebirth is another name for death.

Death is a natural cycle of life and evolution.
Death comes in many forms and does not need to be scary.
It is only scary because it is unknown.
The unknown is where you insert the boogie man and let your mind run free with irrational possibilities. Death, however, is a straightforward process once you know.

I felt as though I would do you a disservice if I did not talk about the concept of death and afterlife in our time today. Our primary focus will be on the death of emotions, beliefs, and actions; however, I feel your curiosity of human death.

The universe and all its parts and inhabitants are energy.
The human idea and the way you think of matter and physicality are incorrect.
Not the science, but the way you believe physical objects are immovable if they are too large. If everything is energy, all things can be changed and be affected by other energies.
If everything is energy, then your physical body is energy (think of atoms-particles).
All these atoms are moving at different speeds and that is the difference between solid, liquid, and gas.

A human like you has multiple layers of energy around and through you.
Your physical body – think cells and atoms.
Your soul – individual to you, woundable, energy.
Your consciousness – energy, expanded you, contains your soul,

your frequency or vibration, shared with limited others.

The human collective consciousness – a thought freeway all humans share.

All these factors affect and influence you and your energy.

When you die, your soul and consciousness leave the physical body.

You disassociate from your body.

The death experience will be different for everyone.

At the moment of death, whatever you believe will happen, will happen.

Do you believe angels or deceased loved ones will greet you and you will walk through a tunnel of light? That is what will happen.

Do you believe there will be two doors? One to heaven and one to hell? That is what will happen.

Do you believe you are going to hell no matter what? To suffer and burn for eternity if you walk into the light? Why would you walk into the light? Many do not, for many reasons, and they become disassociated souls or ghosts.

These ghosts are the soul and consciousness of the person, not the physical body.

Remember free will; you always have a choice.

Once someone crosses into the light, they are connected with the highest versions of their soul. They are aware of all the energy and vibrational happenings of the universe. They can still visit Earth as a spirit, but they have a greater understanding of the world and purpose.

Now that we have talked about death, what is the meaning of life?

What is the meaning of life itself?

What is the meaning of human life?

What is the meaning of your life?

These fundamental questions have been asked for millennia, by all races, beliefs, and sects.

The higher brain function of man needs to have a purpose for its being, society, and systems. Purpose is a difficult construct when you do not have a full understanding of the system you are within.

What is your life?

Your life is a series of events stringed together in your mind – events that shape your understanding of the world.

What about everything else in-between that you forget about?

Do events slip away from your mind forever or do they create a tapestry of life?

Humans place so much emphasis on big events that they miss the small nuances of life.

These small events make up most of your time here on Earth.

I tell you these things so you can change the way you see your life.

Do not live for the big moments; see the small ones as just as important because they make up who you are.

The beauty of life is your mind's ability to see the life you live.

Your mind, and its many facets, allows you to store memories, create, imagine, and do complex physical tasks. Your mind holds not only the knowledge of your current life, but all other lives that you have lived here on Earth and other planets as well.

Take care of your mind much like you take care of your body.

Nourish it and clean out the closets of negativity.

Release negative emotions and habits.

Your unconscious mind is created from your childhood experiences and rules your life, and many have not learned to change it.

Why is your unconscious mind in control? This is because of your human wiring.

How do you overwrite, override, and change these patterns?
1. Recognize your behaviors and thoughts (these behaviors and thoughts served you at one time, but possibly no longer).
2. Believe you can change. Believe you have the power to change your thoughts.
3. Stop behaviors and thought patterns you no longer desire.

Why is it so important to recognize automatic patterns and thoughts that are stored in the unconscious mind that controls one's life?

Understanding your core beliefs are important on many levels:
1. Negative thoughts, experiences, and traumas can create a loop of unhealthy beliefs that do not bring you to joy and happiness.
2. You cannot create real change in your life without knowing what is controlling your actions from your unconscious mind.
3. Your society has taught you to disbelieve yourself, your abilities, and what your physical and energetic body is capable of.

Without changing your unconscious beliefs around energy and abilities, you will always be limited in what you can do energetically and spiritually.

Letting go of that which no longer serves you will allow you to call forth that which you desire.

Letting go can be scary as you are taught to fear the unknown. What if you can let go and call in divine change, knowing that all that happens to you is bringing you to your highest, most divine self? This will take practice and faith, but it helps to know that the path you are calling forth is beautiful, kind, and greater than anything you can conceptualize. You only need to wade out of the mud to find it. As you wade, fight through and change, you also heal, grow, and expand into a fuller version of you, and call forth your soul to be a greater presence in your life.

Do not fear the unknown. Walk into this change with excitement for who you are and who you can become – the full authentic you.

*REBIRTH ACTIVATION

Take a moment to get comfortable. Possibly light a candle, put on soothing music or ear plugs, and find an eye cover. Intend for your divine and enlightened protector beings to surround you as you move into this activation. Know that you are safe and only that which brings you to the New Earth can happen to you.

Breathe deeply through your nose and release the breath slowly. Do this as many times as you need to get into a deeply relaxed state.

Imagine you are in an expansive field with tall grass swaying in the breeze. You touch the tips of the stocks and feel the rough texture on your fingertips. The sun is bright, but not hot, bringing a dry earthy smell. The breeze rustles the grass and creates a light swooshing sound that feels comforting and safe.

As you walk through the field, feeling carefree and enjoying this moment, you feel a pull within your heart that the time of change is upon you. You feel ready to let go of all that is holding you back from living your soul-filled life. You drop to your knees and dig a shallow hole.

You place your hands on your heart and say, **"Dear Great Creator, I thank you for this human life, these human experiences, and my human mind. I am ready to release the densities I carry to move into my divine mind, divine life, and divine purpose. I thank you for creating a clear path forward into the life of my dreams filled with love, joy, and purpose."**

You move your hands from your heart towards the ground as small orbs of light fall from your hands into the hole. More orbs fall from your body and move into the shallow hole and disappear into the soil. You let go again, possibly knowing and choosing what you are releasing and giving permission to release. You watch as everything you are ready to release leaves your physical form, joining the Earth.

You feel warm sunshine on your back as you continue to let go. You know this light – the light of divine love – is wrapping you in a blanket of warmth and comfort. Each orb is a thought, an emotion, a relationship, a trauma, a hurtful word, or a limiting belief.

Tears fall from your face as you get deeper into the pain, hurt, and trauma of your human life. It is time to release all that you hold that is no longer serving you and does not bring you to the New Earth. You are ready to let it all go.

As you release more, you become increasingly aware of the light gathering around and inside of you. As you let go, you welcome more divine light within you – the divine light of love, of Source, and of your divine soul. You welcome the light and ask it to fill more of you.

You continue to release and fill until you feel a sense of completion in your heart. You move from the old version into the new expanded version of you with new potential, new opportunities, and a new path forward.

When you are ready, thank the Earth for taking your pain, sadness, and hurt. Feel gratitude in your heart for the wisdom of knowing this release is available to you. You close the shallow hole and feel the new frequencies you hold in your body. You feel at peace and wrapped in a divine blanket of love.
Take some time to sit quietly and reflect on your experience.

This activation can be done many times and it will continue to go deeper into your energy body each time it is completed. You must be ready for the changes and be ready to release what you are letting go. As you continue to release, you will become more aware of what is ready to surface, be healed, and released. **This is a cycle, not a straight line.**

You will repeat the process of letting go of your old self many times to emerge new. You hold many layers of consciousness, frequencies, and pain. It will take many cycles to allow your divine soul to shine through to be your full authentic self, to shine bright within your human form.

SURRENDER

Dive into the depths of your soul to release your true potential and being.
Create freedom to be authentically you.
Let's start with this question: What is surrender in the context of soul work?
Is it letting go? Trusting the universe? Or leaping and knowing a net will appear?
Turns out that all of these are true – kind of, but not exactly.

Surrender is a concept that is completely foreign to most Western cultures. Why? You are taught to control. You are taught to control your life, your actions, your success, and those around you to create what you want.

Let's take a deeper dive into surrender to reframe your need to control your lives.
Let's move into freedom to create, guide, and flow into what you choose.
Be authentically you and create the internal safety to let all of you shine.

Currently, your idea of surrender is letting go, which in some ways is accurate, but also not accurate.

You hold too tight to the concept of creation and micro creation.

You visualize and live in the details of your dreams.

Yet, you hold onto those details as the only way.

There is a fine balance between living in the details, feeling and experiencing the dream, and accepting new details. **Nothing is set in stone, so allow your dreams to be fluid.**

Surrender is a trust, a knowingness, and a balance of creation and desire that you have not fully grasped yet.

Surrender is a concept that has been broken by your culture and most people walking the world will struggle with surrender because it is too vulnerable.

Other cultures are able to surrender willingly, but not yours.

Surrender is not merely letting go and hoping what you desire returns to you.

It is more than letting the universe allow the creation.

Surrender is the trust and faith deep inside you; it is the embrace of your guides and cradle of trust and protection.

You do not even have words for what this is because you do not trust others that deeply.

You do not allow others to control the world you live in.

You are taught YOU must control all aspects, people, thoughts, actions, and outcomes of your life.

A tree does not know its location when planted, it does not calculate the distance to a stream, yet the Earth is covered in massive, beautiful trees.

Blind faith is also a concept that is a misunderstanding as well.

Throwing up your arms and letting go does not manifest what you desire.

(We will apply steps on what to do next. This is complicated and not an easy state to be in, yet once you arrive, it is freedom.)

Your culture teaches you to work hard to create your dreams. You are driven to try and try again. You are defined by your success and the amount of control you have over your life – schedules, bills, and obligations.

Surrender is another word for trust. Trust yourself, trust those around you, and trust the universe will provide by doing what you love and enjoy.

SAFETY
Start with safety: Do you feel safe, and do you trust yourself?

• Feel into that emotion and statement

• Do you feel safe?

• Do you trust yourself to do what is best for you? Or do what is best for the family or within what is expected of you?

• Do you even ask yourself what you want, and do you listen?

How do you surrender to the universe when you do not feel safe and you don't trust yourself?
This is the dilemma today.

CONTROL
Control and the need for control must be released – control of your surroundings, control of your thoughts, and control of the unexpected.

• What do you believe you need to control in your life to be safe? Or feel safe to be you?

• The neighborhood you need to live in, the education you have, or the way you look and behave?

• How do you allow others to treat you? Are you fighting for a voice and to be heard? Or a need to be recognized?

Upon reflection of these items, how do you move into surrender? First you must feel safe – safe in your body, safe in your mind, and safe to be authentically you (even if it is just inside your mind). Second, you must realize, work through, and accept that you truly have no control.

You can guide, drive, maneuver, and create, but ultimately control is a mental construct you created in your brain. The more you wish to control versus guide, the harder this will be.

The tighter you hold on, the more resistance and struggle you create.

By guiding, you understand there are variables you do not see. Yet, you walk confidently forward, knowing these obstacles, mistakes, choices, and other people's choices will come into play and will be navigated. You know you will gracefully incorporate these changes into your plan. These changes may push you out of your comfort zone at times; however, you must know it will work out. Possibly not how you planned, but how it is intended to be.

Expecting change and the unexpected will put you in a mind space of creativity and opportunity. This also keeps your mind elastic and creates a greater sense of confidence as you navigate situations.

What is one aspect or activity in your life you can practice? What do you desire that you can move into trusting yourself 100 percent?
Let's practice on an example of traffic while driving to work or school.

Let's start with manifesting what you want:
• Manifestation: What do you want? A smooth drive to or from work that is relaxing.
• What are your roadblocks? What needs to be released?

Identify your roadblocks to change thoughts, fears, beliefs, frustrations, anxiety, thoughts of being late, or feeling like it is wasting your time, etc.

- Call in – ease, relaxation, smooth flowing traffic that allows for a quick commute.
- Visualize – feel the relaxing drive with traffic moving smoothly.
- Surrender

Surrender the drive to the universe. Start by saying a few of the following:

- I feel safe in my car as other cars move gracefully around me.
- I am protected in my actions and movements.
- The universe is creating the optimum environment for my drive.
- I am in the flow.
- I release anything and everything that is not grace and ease.
- I release and let go. I trust and move into gratitude.

To start, you might have to say the above sentences 10 to 20 times in a car ride. After a couple days, you might get to decrease this number. This may take weeks to months to change your thoughts and emotions, so be patient with the process. This is how you overwrite your prior autopilot with a new one. Change your thoughts to change your experience.

You will change the frequency you emit.
You will change the scenarios presented.
You will start to see and feel changes being created, which builds trust.
You can then expand into other scenarios and situations.

Move into freedom to create, guide, and flow in what you choose. Be authentically you and create the internal safety to let all of you shine.

*SURRENDER ACTIVATION

Take a moment to get comfortable. Possibly light a candle, put on soothing music or ear plugs, and find an eye cover. Intend for your divine and enlightened protector beings to surround you as you move into this activation. Know that you are safe and only that which brings you to the New Earth can happen to you.

Breathe deeply through your nose and release the breath slowly. Do this as many times as you need to get into a deeply relaxed state.

You are standing on the edge of a beautiful waterfall. You have been hiking in the woods and stopped to watch a large river flowing from the cascading falls. There is a mist that gathers with prisms of dancing light, and you hear the crash of the water falling to the Earth.

You lose your footing and fall into the river below the falls. You swim towards the surface, surprised, shocked, scared, and cold. Your head emerges above the water, and you gasp for air. The cold creeps into your muscles making it hard to move.

The current is strong, so you are unable to swim to shore from this location. You float on your back, pointing your feet downstream and center yourself and breathe, then release...

You breathe in deeply, letting your lungs expand with air, then release slowly, and repeat.
It is only you and the water at this moment.
You let the fear, shock, and adrenaline move from your veins into the rushing waters around you. There is chaos, fear, the unknown, and busyness happening around you, much like your life, pulling at you from all sides. So, you release it. Let it go. Breathe through the release. You feel the water rushing past, pushing you to and fro'. You let go of the desire to control.
You realize you have no control at this moment. You surrender so you

can call the calm from within you.

You let go of control.

You let go of expectations.

You are alert – watching and choosing, but not fighting nor controlling.

You breathe again to find your inner calm.

You feel the water slow down, but the current is still too strong, so you continue to let go and release all fear and panic into the water. You look up towards the sky to see the bright Sun in the sky and you can feel warm sun rays on your face.

You know this light. It is more than the sun; it is the protection of divine love and Source. You tell yourself you are protected and guided. You pull in the divine light, but also feel your own light rise within you. You are ready for anything that lies ahead – you have the skills, the know-how, and ability to face any situation.

You pull up your inner strength to feel confidence in this powerless situation, asking for protections, guidance, and the most divine outcome.

You build a sense of safety and strength from within you. You have the skills and tools to succeed, to thrive – you only need to ask, be guided, release your fears, and call on the strength from within.

You feel a small bump on your feet and realize you gently hit something. Looking down you see the river pushed you into a gentle pool by the shore. Your feet hit the sandy beach, so you pull yourself out of the water to lay on the sand. As you lay there, you connect with the Sun, the Earth and Source.

You reflect on your experience of the rushing water and how similar you are caught in the busyness and demands of modern life. Sometimes feeling like you can barely come up to breathe between work, kids, sports, family obligations or other's expectations of you.

By letting go and not allowing the chaos to take over, you take back guiding the direction of your own life.

You asked for divine guidance and protections.

You released your fear and need for control.

You called on your inner strength and knowingness that you are ready and prepared for anything that is ahead of you. Call on this strength and knowingness when you need to find your inner peace when the chaos of life rages around you.

When you feel complete, bring your mind back to your physical body and mind, and feel the accomplishment of letting go and asking your strength to rise from within.

Take some time to sit quietly and notice the subtle changes taking place.

GROUNDING

Message from Mother Earth:
Grounding your energy into the Earth is more than just a connection, it is an exchange.
An exchange of energy, information, healing and knowing.
Why connect? You are an earthly being who was designed to walk barefoot on my surface. We exchange information when there is a connection.
What information? Healings, releases, uplifting thoughts. We were always meant to be connected continuously and not in small snippets of time. I will ask for you to connect, to receive information and attune our frequencies.
Many Blessings upon you my dear.
-Mother Earth (Gaia)

You must go as deep below as you rise above.
If you only increase your connections with the higher frequencies without intentionally grounding, you become lopsided. It is critical to have a conscious practice of grounding as you do energy work.

Grounding, or the act of energetically tethering your energy to the Earth as you explore energetic spaces, protects you and serves you in many ways.
You are first and foremost an energetic being experiencing a human life.
You are connected to a physical body, but your soul and consciousness are navigating the Energy and Spirit realms. The act of grounding is important to call yourself home to your physical form and to be healed by Mother Earth.

Our Mother Earth is a beautiful soul who is here to help you along your physical body's journey. She has a very special gift and purpose to transmute energy into her divine frequency.
By giving her your anger, frustration, hurt and pain, she can transmute it into something beautiful and healing.

The act of connecting is simple yet energetically profound.
Today, I ask you to practice grounding, as well as release.
Grounding provides the vessel of healing, information, and exchange to take place with Mother Earth. You will initially travel to the center of the Earth (energetic center) to meet Gaia and create anchor points within the Earth's core.

I would like you to picture yourself standing in the yard of your home.
Visualize your toes in the soil and energetic roots descending from your feet.
These roots may begin small but become larger and denser.
The roots go to the center of the Earth and wrap around her core.

You can feel the energy of the Earth travel back to you along the roots – the healing frequencies of nature, the vibration of the peaceful forest or the slow lapping waves at the beach.

There are many ways to connect and release. You can use the elements of the Earth to help connect with her.

How do you connect best with Mother Earth? With earth, water, fire, or air?
· With your feet in the soil?
· Gazing into a beautiful bonfire?
· Floating in a lake or ocean?
· Standing at a mountain top and visualizing the emotions as they're pulled from you by the wind?

You can explore these on your own. Work with each element to find your desired way to release.

We release to make room for what we desire in our lives.
Let your mind travel to what you seek to release and let go.

Release the things you do not wish to keep. The things that hold you back from your true potential and keep you from your happiness.

*GROUNDING ACTIVATION

The New Earth is an important ally as you expand your vibrational quality. Many expect to expand their consciousness into the higher consciousness only; however, there must be an equal depth to the vibrational reach. One must go as deep as they go high to remain balanced. Connecting deep into the core of the Earth allows your mind to expand farther into the expansion of all.

Take a moment to get comfortable. Possibly light a candle, put on soothing music or ear plugs, and find an eye cover. Intend for your divine and enlightened protector beings to surround you as you move into this activation. Know that you are safe and only that which brings you to the New Earth can happen to you.

Breathe deeply through your nose and release the breath slowly. Do this as many times as you need to get into a deeply relaxed state.

Visualize walking in a densely wooded forest. Smell the fresh earth under your feet as a soft breeze brings aromas of flowers and clear crisp air. Feel the gentle breeze as you go deeper into your imagination. Breathe deeply and visualize.

See a clear forest path before you as you gracefully stroll forward. There is a large ancient oak tree that commands the forest space. You walk towards the old oak and place your hands on her rough bark.

You can feel the depth of wisdom this tree holds. You place your forehead on her trunk and find your focus slipping into the flow of the oak tree. You feel her energy and movement pulling you down into her roots.

There is an elaborate system of roots that move through the soil and damp earth. You find yourself following the roots deeper and deeper into the Earth, eventually leaving the roots behind and finding your focus pulled to the center of the energetic Earth.

Visualize yourself floating within the depths of the Earth, creating a solid anchor point. The Earth's soft embrace holds you as you connect and explore. Allow your logical mind to release and expand into the space around you. Release and let go of what you are ready to let go, and give to the Earth all that you are ready to let go.

Stay in this space as long as you feel comfortable, then return to your body at the base of the oak tree. Know you can reconnect to the anchors and energetic signatures anytime. Feel yourself firmly anchored as you return to the tree. Tell her thank you and lay gifts at her feet (water, crystals, flowers, or gratitude) and then walk slowly down the path, returning to your physical body and mind.

INDIVIDUALITY

Individuality is the misguided concept of being alone. You are not alone. Your physical body has independence, and you have an individual mind and soul; however, those aspects are not truly alone. You are a multidimensional being with your soul represented many times on this planet. Let's not forget the many consciousnesses you share.

You are energetically tethered to each human, animal, plant, and this planet. The farther into the belief of individuality you travel, the more secluded you become. As you alienate yourself, you cut off your connection with Source. By allowing your connection with Source to grow and become stronger, you allow connections with all living beings to flourish. You will see yourself as part of the whole and not a single piece as you grow energetically.

The New Earth is a place of collectivity, harmony, and connection. One must shed the concept that advancing one person will bring change that is good for all.

The free flow of thoughts, information, and teachings is what will create the harmonious society of the future. One person cannot stand alone in a sea of humans to create change.
Rather, one person can teach, share, and grow with a sea of humans to create change.

Change is upon you, and it is time to learn and grow. It is time to learn how to connect with the collective – to see and connect beyond you. It is time to find ways to give to others, to share thoughts, love, food, and time.

Money is not always the answer.

Expand your concept of you to include more than your physical form.

DANCE WITH SHADOW

Connecting to Source and understanding your oneness (your connection with everything) is an important steppingstone of awakening and enlightenment. You are more than an individual person; you are part of an expanded energetic system within and around you.

Integrating into the energetic system of Source energy and oneness will assist you in expanding beyond you and calling forth all of you.

Oneness is not only the connection with everything, but also the soul's dance with the light and shadow. You cannot be whole without honoring your shadow and its teachings.

Shadow is another name for the densities you carry and lessons learned by these experiences.

You become the person you are intended to be because of shadow. Shadow has an important job of presenting options and creating desires and struggles that help you learn what you do and do not want in your life.

The dance with shadow is an important milestone of ascension.

A balanced dance is a balanced life.

If you only live in the light, you will not grow.

By creating a relationship with and respect for your shadow, you allow the dance to begin.

You will begin to heal in a new way, understanding the pain you carry brought you to this point in your life and who you are today.

Honor your dance partner for it has an important role in creating your dream life.

ONENESS

You are surrounded by energies, spirits, and forces you do not yet understand.

To start properly playing the game of life, you need to understand the energetic rules.

You are currently walking blindly without a compass, map, or instructions.

It is hard to succeed with missing pieces. Come learn the rules of the energetic world to thrive, succeed, and build the life of your dreams.

Start by connecting to the energetic system and understanding energies around you.

This system is vast and never ending, so start with you and the nature around you.

Step into the flow of oneness to become all of you and to have access to all the human abilities, understanding, and knowledge that are flowing to this beautiful planet.

Oneness is a connection with Source, a connection with your soul, and a connection with everything else.

Oneness is the flow of life, energy, and awareness around you – how you affect others and how others effect you.

Once you tap into the flow of oneness, you expand your ability to tap into yourself, your abilities, and the stream of information your mind constantly receives from the energetic world around you.

Oneness is more than a state.

It is more than information.

It is more than a connection to the cosmos with its infinite possibilities and creation.

It is all of this and more.

Oneness is a natural ability everyone possesses.
You are already connected to the energetic web that surrounds you. While you may not know, understand, or consciously interpret the information, your mind, body, and unconscious mind does.

How do you knowingly tap into the expanded consciousness of "oneness?"
By creating the desire and intention.
To begin, you must ask to connect and to be one with spirit, the whole of you, and whole knowledge.

Visualize your oneness as God (universal consciousness, Source, etc.) breathing his divine breath over you, illuminating you with healing, information, wisdom, possibility, opportunity, and unconditional love.

This breath can be caught, harnessed, and understood.
How do you catch the wind?
You catch the wind by aligning frequencies, by listening to your knowingness, and learning how to hear the messages given.
You will be guided to an interpretation and to follow the feelings that arise within you.
As you learn and grow, the interpretations, understanding, and meanings will evolve.
All will be done and revealed in a timing that is perfect for you.

You are meant to do more.
You were always meant to be more.
Ask to receive your gifts in a loving and divine way that will teach you with grace.

The 'you' who sits here today will not be the same 'you' who will sit here tomorrow.

Not only because of the information you now hold but the additional breaths, thoughts, choices, and decisions made. You are ever evolving, even when you feel like you are standing still.

Standing still is still a choice and frequency.
The world will change frequency tomorrow.
There is never the same moment, and as you step into the flow of oneness, you will perceive the changes around you differently.
Believe that you are here today at the right time and place to receive and understand this message.

*ONENESS ACTIVATION

Take a moment to get comfortable. Possibly light a candle, put on soothing music or ear plugs, and find an eye cover. Intend for your divine and enlightened protector beings to surround you as you move into this activation. Know that you are safe and only that which brings you to the New Earth can happen to you.

Breathe deeply through your nose and release the breath slowly. Do this as many times as you need to get into a deeply relaxed state.

We revisit our friend, the ancient oak tree. As you approach, you can smell the fresh Earth under your feet and the soft wind bringing aromas of flowers and clear crisp air.
Feel a gentle breeze as you move deeper into your imagination.
Breathe deeply and visualize.

See a forest path before you as you gracefully stroll towards the ancient oak.
You touch her rough bark and greet her like an old friend. As you connect and say hello, you place your forehead on her trunk and feel your mind move into the oak's large trunk.

Move your awareness up towards the sky. Feel the expansive branches with their strength, then move to smaller flexible limbs, and eventually into the leaves.

You can feel the expansive life within the tree and how alive she is.

There is water rushing from the ground to her leaves, her sap pumps like blood bringing nutrients to her farthest limbs, and there are colonies of insects that travel her trunk.

As you settle farther into the feeling of the tree, you notice something within you open, allowing a deeper connection to begin. Simultaneously, you feel the tree's leaves, roots, and life within and round the tree. You expand. You feel all of her at once.

As you move into more leaves, you feel yourself being pulled to the tree next door – you are now within the leaves of both trees. You travel down the neighboring tree's trunk to connect with the soil. You see and feel the ancient oak's roots twist and turn within the neighboring tree's network of roots. There is an overlap, a sharing and kinship between the two trees.

Your mind is being pulled along the forest floor to all of life: Insects, animals, fungi, roots, leaves, and saplings. You feel connected and are consciously able to bounce between many of these beings. There is a gentle flow of familiarity, kinship, and symbiosis – a gentleness and ease amongst all life.

You are omnipresent and able to move with the beings of the forest surrounding the oak. Feel yourself expand, not only your mind but your awareness and ability to simultaneously connect with all the spirits and beings within the forest floor.

The oneness is all encompassing, connecting into all that is possible and all that is divine.

The expansion of consciousness moves within and around you, welcoming you to return and feel the presence of all. The divine love and connection that flows through all living and non-living objects here on Earth.

You begin to contract your expanded mind and call back all pieces of you. When you feel whole, thank this beautiful, divine forest for sharing her life with you. You leave gifts on the forest floor with gratitude and return to the path, then to your body and mind.

LOVE & FEAR

Love and fear hold the same vibrational intensity but on opposite ends of the vibrational spectrum.

The emotions you feel and thoughts you create will create your personal frequency.

When you live in fear and allow your mind to propagate fearful emotions, you pull more fear towards you.

Love
Oneness
Grounding
Surrender
Rebirth
Manifestation
Release, Heal

You have both love and fear inside of you. What you choose to focus on is what grows.

Do you choose to grow more love in your life? Or do you grow more fear?

How can you change your current life to include more love?

Start with yourself and grow your self-love.
Start within.
When you live in self-love, you have an infinite source of love to work with and expand from. You are not dependent on another or another's belief system and actions.

How do you grow self-love?
I want you to see yourself the way your spirit guides do.

I want to show you the amount of love, support, and reverence we have for you.

You are doing the hard work on Earth, and we are so proud of you.

Feel – Connect – Allow

Take a moment to take a couple deep breaths and ask your spirit allies to show you how much you are loved. Feel into them with your heart.

Breathe and feel.

Ask to be shown how much you are loved.

Move into your heart space to feel the love flowing to you from within and the spirits around you.

Breathe and feel.

I want you to feel this way from the inside out.

I want you to hold yourself, your desires, beliefs, and purpose on a pedestal knowing you and they are important.

Your culture teaches you to care for others and put yourself last. There needs to be a balance between your needs and others. Neither extreme is good for you. By giving too much of yourself, you deplete your stores of energy, love, and time. Finding balance is important.

Much of the current human's mental conditioning needs to be examined and healed.

Some of you will need outside help (example: therapy, reconditioning, support groups, etc.) to move through the blocks while others can do this by examining thoughts and emotions on their own.

How do you change thoughts and emotions? Recognition, choice, and reconditioning.

Find what facades you carry that teach you how to behave and believe (cultural, family, personal belief systems).

Recognize your belief system, choose what you want to believe, then recondition your thought patterns.

Most people have limiting thoughts. Search for these limiting thoughts and ask, "Why do I believe this?"
Break down these beliefs to establish what to heal.

Writing exercise

What is one of your fears, or limiting beliefs?
Example: Sharing my gifts, teaching, or standing in front of people.
Why?
Example: Fear of being judged, saying something wrong or not believed.
Why does this scare you?
Example: Being pushed out, not accepted by others, or believed. Made to feel small.
Why does this affect you? What is the root fear?
Example: Not being accepted or believed
How do you change this?
Example: Believe in your inner voice. Trust. Knowing your path and calling.
What is the root belief causing fear? Fear of not belonging. A basic human need that feels threatened. This root belief is what must be healed.

Take time to be vulnerable with yourself as you explore these questions to understand what is holding you back.
Recognition gives you the power to choose and to change;
without understanding what you believe, you can never choose.

LOVE IS THE LANGUAGE OF YOUR SOUL

Love is the language and frequency of your soul.

Your soul recognizes love within another when you connect on a soul level.

Love, light, and frequency are the building blocks of the future.

This future is so bright it is blinding to the human eyes.

Your human eyes see a very limited spectrum of light.

Light waves expand beyond what you see into a cascade of language and technology that is to come. By building your technologies with light, you build a sustainable and infinite future – infinite with technological advances in time, space, matter, and frequency.

Love is the frequency of your soul and is the frequency of God, Source, and the infinite.

How can the soul be a frequency of light, sound, vibration, and how can all these frequencies align in harmony?

How does Source connect and flow through all things? Light, sound, and vibration.

How does the human body communicate with other cells? Light, sound, and vibration.

How do you connect with other people? Light, sound, and vibration.

What are you at the core? Light, sound, and vibration.

Why do I repeat these things? Because you do not see humans or yourself in this way.

What would change if you did?

You would change.

You would see yourself as part of the whole. Within a system, not separate and alone.

Pull your view of yourself into a view with the world and universe.
Love is the language of your soul – it is who you are at your core
and infinite being.
Love, we recognize within and for others.

Love, we have for ourselves.
Love, we have for the planet, her abundance of life, and the life
sustenance she provides.
Love for the Mother – your own Mother, your Mother Earth, and
your Spiritual Mother.
Who is your Spiritual Mother? Who has nurtured, guided,
protected, and healed you?
Come meet her and the love that pours from her heart for you, all
that you are, and all that you can be and ever were.
You are so deeply loved in more ways than you will ever
understand.

There are not enough words to describe love.
The love you have for yourself, your children, spouse, job, and
objects is not the same type of love.
Yet, we do not have another word for this intense human emotion.

What is love? How do you feel love?
Did you know your body produces different chemicals and
hormones based on the different types of love? Your human body
was designed to live in the frequency of love, which is different
than the emotion of love.

The emotion of love, this you understand.
The frequency of love is a wavelength, this you understand.
The actions of love, this you understand.
What about a BEING of love? This you do not understand.

I Am love.
You are a being of love.

What does that mean? It means your physical form is hardwired to know, understand, and recognize love.

Your soul is the frequency of love. When you're not in physical form, you live in the frequency of love.

How do you move the frequency of love into your whole being and life?

You start by reconnecting you, your soul, and your connection with Source.

*LOVE ACTIVATION

The Spiritual Mother – who is she?

She is your guardian angel. She is a beacon in the dark, and she is your gentle comfort.

She is many and all things, but most importantly, she is your guiding light of Awakening.

Meeting the Spiritual Mother, does many things:
- She can heal wounds, traumas, and blocks
- She can upgrade your energy and chakra system
- She can reconnect your inner voice
- She can realign your understanding of the world and your place in it
- She can set you free

There is something special about a mother's love.

It is unconditional, nurturing, and life sustaining – it is a breath of fresh air.

Today, we meet the Spiritual Mother, and she has gifts for you. She is here to help you on your spiritual journey.

What questions do you have for her? Below are a few questions that can support you in creating your own to ask the Mother.

- What is holding me back from living my dreams?
- What limiting beliefs do I hold that prevents me from living a life with more joy and happiness?
- What do I need to release / heal / learn to live my life's purpose?
- How do I expand into all that I am that I cannot yet see?

Let the Spiritual Mother guide you towards your dreams and your purpose.
Let her shower you with gifts and love to help you move forward with your dreams.

Your Spiritual Mother awaits your arrival and welcomes you with open arms in the Banquet Hall of the Spiritual Mother. You will create your own experience in this activation. Open your imagination to all that you are and will be.

Take a moment to get comfortable. Possibly light a candle, put on soothing music or ear plugs, and find an eye cover. Intend for your divine and enlightened protector beings to surround you as you move into this activation. Know that you are safe and only that which brings you to the New Earth can happen to you.

Breathe deeply through your nose and release the breath slowly. Do this as many times as you need to get into a deeply relaxed state.

You are walking along a gravel path with a rhythmic, soft crunch beneath your feet. You see a building ahead made of gray stone with large arching windows and ornately carved wooden doors. You pull open the doors to find a banquet hall filled with elaborate decorations that exude the feeling of warmth and welcome.

There is a lone woman standing in the hall. You greet her warmly, introduce yourself, and you respectfully exchange gifts.

You hold out your hands to find you have an object heavy in your palm. (Feel into it, do you know what it is? What does it look and feel like?)

You lovingly offer her your gift.

She then bestows a gift upon you. Can you feel, see, or know what your gift is? It could be a blessing, healing, object, or wisdom bestowed upon you.

There is always an exchange, even when you do not know the details. You can ask questions to find out more if you are unsure. You may hear, see, or know the answer.

When the exchange is complete, thank her for your gifts and respectfully place your hands on your heart to welcome a heart-to-heart connection.

You turn to the oak doors and down the gravel path, knowing you can return and visit your new friend at any time.

EXISTENCE

Existence ... what does that mean?
Who are you and what are you referring to?
What does existence on the physical plane you are within mean?
What does existence within the physical body you are within mean?
What does existence within the timeline, dimension, and reality that you currently live mean?
What do all these things mean?

What does existence mean when you live within an understanding of a world that is limited and without the whole picture of who you truly are?

Existence is a difficult place to be.
Existence is infinite.
You exist on an infinite timeline because your soul is infinite.

What does this mean? This means that the essence of your soul was created when the universe was created. You return to the cosmos, or the heavens as you like to call them, when you are not in earthly form. You are also located in many physical bodies that are currently living on the Earth. You are within many animals, plants, rays of light, and other objects or beings, because that is how your soul and consciousness exist to experience life and purpose.

In addition to being on Earth, you are on other planets with intelligent life and non-intelligent life. You are also present in the ethereal worlds, where councils meet, souls gather, and we create and co-create. Your ability to be in many of these places at the same time exists because that is how your soul and consciousness were developed. It was developed to experience many things and to gain experiences and understanding of the worlds around them.

I hope this book creates a new understanding of your soul and consciousness, as well of your earthly life and purpose.

The purpose now for humans, if they so choose, is to become enlightened.
Is to move into the next phase of human evolution.
Human evolution is human enlightenment.
Human enlightenment begins with awakening.

It begins with the call to your own soul to be present and forefront in your physical body – to connect with the frequency of your consciousness and to wake up the cells of your body and bathe them in the light and frequency of your consciousness.

I welcome you to experience these things so you can choose the path before you. However, without an understanding of your choices, you walk a blinded life.

Wake up to the New Earth – to an Earth that values love and togetherness, collectivity, joy and all the freedoms of the mental, emotional, and physical that are allotted to you here on Earth.

Understand the gifts you are given in this physical body.
Understand you are limitless in what you can do.
Remove the limiting beliefs you have placed on your mind.

Allow your mind to expand beyond you and beyond this physical form.
Allow your mind to reach into the Earth and into other souls to connect, enlighten, and be one.
Allow your mind to experience full support and love – unconditional love – for those around you while also radiating it from within you.

Love is the goal.
Love is the experience you are seeking.
Wake up to your possibilities to walk forward into your new life and into the New Earth.

NEXT PHASE

The time of awakening is upon you.
The time of action is upon you.
The time of becoming who you are and who you are meant to be is upon you.
Those seeking the light of truth will allow Source into their hearts, follow their path, explore their humanity, heal their wounds, and leap into the New Earth.

The New Earth is here for you to explore.
The New Earth is present today and many live there now in the frequency of love, joy, and acceptance.

They understanding there are battles raging around them within the Old Earth and the gray space of decision, yet those things cannot touch them.

Wars cannot touch those living in the New Earth because there is no vibrational alignment.

Unfortunately, the wars, struggle, and chaos will continue to build, and those living in chaos will continue to have to choose. Your choice is to succumb to chaos, pain, and fear or choose to pursue happiness, joy, and freedom.

It seems like an easy choice from this vantage point; however, when you are amid pain and suffering, this is a very hard decision. This is a hard path to take.

We want to make it easy.

We want to make it as graceful as possible.

However, we honor your free will and your ability to decide.

We honor your ability to follow your heart and your desires. If that does not include us, then we cannot help you.

I ask that you feel into your heart.

Feel into your soul and the depth of your heart space. Who are you? What are you meant to be doing? Who are you meant to be? Let that expand and grow inside of your heart, your soul, your mind.

Follow the whisperings, the knowingness, and the ease of the path. This will lead you to your awakening, your enlightenment, and to your freedom.

I do not say these things about change to bring fear. I say these things because they are the reality of the Earth that has been chosen by the humans upon it.

I say this from a place of unfortunate circumstance.

I want every person on Earth to ascend to the place they desire – whether that is the New or Old Earth.

I desire freedom.
I desire choice.
I desire honoring your free will.

The time of mass awakening is upon us.
It is being taught and spread by many great teachers who came with the purpose to awaken the humans currently residing on Earth.

They came to awaken and give options and choices.
They came to allow those who choose to evolve their souls and consciousnesses to the next level of being and possibility into a new world of different technology, graceful harmony, and symbiosis with the planet.

Future civilizations evolved from the current population on Earth and include those who chose to evolve to the New Earth, those who chose to transcend the current world. They evolved into peaceful people who are highly intelligent with technologies that allow harmony with each other and the planet.
They evolved into a civilization that values life, choice, independence, and collaboration.
These evolved people of the future are here to assist you today.
Time and space are not linear, and everything is happening together.

Allow assistance from those who have a divine, pure intention.
They are here to assist, educate, and give information to allow this process to take place.
They are masters of energy and frequency.
They are masters of interacting with the soul.
They are masters of free will.

The evolution of the New Earth is that of a divine utopia, opportunity, education, and non-judgment.

It is an evolution of the human mind and the awakening, reconnection, and expansion of the soul within the human form.

Your soul resides within you, yet you do not understand what you are capable of. You do not understand how to tap into the knowingness, expansiveness, and abilities of your own soul and the deep connections of your soul to your consciousness and the human collective consciousness. These are all available to you. The abilities are to come by understanding and fostering these connections.

The human mind is a beautiful and expansive place and an untapped place.
It is also a dangerous and harmful place when not allowed to be free, when conditioned to live in fear, and to seek power and control.
When filled with hurt, anger, and the limitations to keep one small, then the human mind is a dangerous place.

To move into the next steps within yourself and within your life, you must choose.
Choose the expansion within you.
Choose the work to get yourself there and act.
Feel what is to come.
Feel what is possible.
Feel not with your physical senses, not with your mind, but with your heart.
Search forward into your heart space – your evolution and your abilities to be so much more are there.

You are meant to be more.
You are meant to feel and understand more.
Remove the limiting thoughts, the limiting beliefs, the limiting concepts that you currently carry. Let the soul within you burn from the inner depths to be present within every cell, every thought, and every action.

Allow your soul to speak.

Allow your divine connection to shine through, to guide you, to expand you, and to teach you who you are – who you are meant to be.
Take action to learn.
Take action to release.
Take action to believe and be.

This is your time - your time of freedom, of awakening, and the pursuit of happiness.

AFTERWORD

As I sit here after writing this book, I am reflecting on all that I have learned about our changing world. I am reflecting on my small place in the world while seeing the bigger picture of the energetic world and the Old Earth amid great change. This change is not outwardly visible but is felt within my heart. It is a change that is sad to feel and heart breaking to experience.

My heart breaks for all the people who are wrapped in the densities of the Old Earth, without understanding how to change their situation, or how to move into the joys that the New Earth offers.

My wish is that everyone has access to this information within this book, the information gifted to me. I am not the owner of these words. They may have come through me; however, they are a gift for all humanity. These words are for those who wish to understand more, for those who have the spark of curiosity, for those who desire to awaken, and for those who wish to pursue enlightenment. I honor all people and where they are at in their lives. I honor everyone's choices, desires, and even their reluctance.

The path that I put before you is not one of simplicity or without pain. The path before you is one of hard work, diligence, change and perseverance. To change your mind, your thoughts, and your unconscious understanding of the world you live in is a complicated undertaking. It is harsh and is compounded by the wounds and traumas from this earthly life and past lives that we must heal.

The purging process can be intense. At times, it can feel like it is easier to give up and many will. This is OK because it is their choice. Many will fight on, and this is OK because it is their choice.

Many will pursue the change they seek within their hearts and the understanding they seek within their minds.

As I sit here, I feel the light of the New Earth and it is brilliant and bright. It is loving and kind. It is welcoming and feels like home. I have worked many years to clear the densities that I carried, not only in my physical body, but my conscious and unconscious mind. Even still, I am not done. I sometimes wonder if we will ever be done. (We are human after all.)

However, my heart and intention are pure. I choose enlightenment. I choose with every cell, every bone, and every energetic fiber of my being to live in this joyful place with the ones I love, and the ones who choose the New Earth. I choose to create a beautiful life of adventure, intrigue, innocence, and joy. At the end of the day, it is me living my dream and sharing my passions and love for this work and pursuit of understanding. My heart bursts with the opportunities and the change that is happening within people. I see the joy it brings them – the opportunity, change and progress. Gifted lives are being created around me and it is humbling and exciting.

It makes me proud.

It makes me proud that I stepped forward when it was hard. It makes me proud of the hard choices I had to make to be successful, to learn, to purge, and to heal. I was scared to put myself out there when others did not understand. In complete transparency, even I did not fully understand what was happening because I only had a small piece of the picture. Yet in my heart, the small piece I had felt so true and so right. I had to face my own insecurities and fears – and I still am, as we all are. We live in a world that thrives on insecurities.

As I heal more and more of myself, I feel more whole, true, and expanded within me. I understand my soul so much better. I understand who she is and what she has come to do. I am fulfilling a longing that I never understood in my younger life, a longing that I desired to figure out, but was just out of my grasp. A longing that was dangled in front of me like a carrot – always out of reach – until now. I have finally walked into an understanding of my purpose, or rather, a small piece of it. I have a clearer understanding of who I am at my eternal core:

I am a teacher.
I am a mentor.
I am a friend.
I am a mother.
I am LOVE.
I am here to show the way to the New Earth.
I am here to show you how to meet your most important teacher, the teacher within yourself.

Serra
August 2022

*Channeled conversation with my True Self

Let me begin with the changes that are upon you – the changes within and without, the changes you must understand and agree to, the changes to your cells, your brain, your abilities, and perceptions ... Do you agree to these changes?

"I agree to fully embody my soul, my soul's purpose and to radiate more of my true self – yes, I agree to these changes if they move me toward my life's purpose and the New Earth's purpose."

Then it is done.

You radiate a new light and love. A new ability to understand, create, and carry. You now transcend your human mind to a place beyond the reach of the Old Earth and its residents. You radiate a new light and love that calls forth more of your human mind. Wrap your body in love as your cells expand and grow to hold more of you. Hold on my dear, you are in for a ride.

To be you is to be many things and many versions, and to hold the light for all. You hold the light for all of mankind who seek the light of divine awakening and knowledge. You call forth the growth, so it expands. You change that which is possible because of what you desire.

"How?" you ask. This is the purpose of your soul. To shake, break down, and rock the foundation of society. You have learned to encompass God's love and possibilities. The expansion within you calls forth the changes to come. Live in your expansion and love and in your growth and change. Embrace chaos because it will surround you as you change more and more in your life and teachings.
Embrace the chaos, surrender to the change, and find joy in your growth.

Be you. Be wholly you. Magnificent, beautiful, and terrifyingly powerful you. Embrace all of you.

How do I expand?

Expand in which way, my dear? Energy, vibration, knowledge, wisdom, abilities, or trust? You are doing all these simultaneously. You are here. Now, just keep walking forward.

What is next?
Change and more change. Buckle up because change is coming

hard and fast. Change in your life, your work, your family, your understanding of self, the universe and life. All you have is change in your next phase. Change you have asked for, created, and approved. Expansion of self, of ability, and of wisdom.

You are a wisdom keeper. A secret keeper of the ancient humans, the Earth, and other planets. You protect the change they seek. You protect the change of the Light. You protect the ability to choose the Light and all that it is.

What is my purpose in this human life?

Your work is beyond you. You are connecting the universal energetic light back into the human physical form. This lost energy was disconnected when humans changed/de-evolved and this was agreed upon by all parties. This agreement also contained the agreement that the light may be re-established, if and when requested. Many people have reconnected their own light and abilities, and there have been other teachers showing how it is done.

You, my dear, are here for the mass reconnection. Your soul is a renegade, an outlier, and a pioneer. You enter to shake things to the core.

Your soul's path is one of mass awakening and enlightenment. You lead the masses with grace and ease to the light of themselves and their joy. You make possible that which was previously impossible. *Why?* I hear in your mind.

That is your soul's purpose. You have done this many times before on this planet and others. You create the opportunity for change. You create the alignment for change, and you light the spark to ignite the change.

You hold a specific purpose within that lovingly spreads through the masses.

This time on Earth, you are bringing in the frequency and teachings to voice the possibilities, hopes, dreams, and realities.

What does that mean in everyday life?

You channel, you teach, you guide, you transform, and you transmute the energies on Earth.
You create a university for souls to learn and grow.
You create content that will unify, awaken, and be digestible for all who choose.
You listen to your guides as they walk you through each step and progression.

You are in the infant state of your work and there is much still unknown to come. You are unsure how this will unfold and what will be created. When you had your children, did you expect to know their personalities and eventual profession? No. This is the same. There are many choices to come regarding the presentation of your work. You will experience and understand different things in each phase, much like your child's personality at different stages. Right now, your focus is on your development, understanding, and channeling basic content.

"What else should you be doing?" you ask.
Why do you feel you are not doing enough? Possibly you are at the exact point, progression, content that you need to be. Will speeding things up get you more? Possibly, or possibly not.

Ask your guides clear questions about your actions, and they will give you clear answers about your direction and tasks. Doing more does not always mean more yield. You will always yield the amount you were intended to.

You are a channel, a conduit. We go at your speed and ability. You will channel almost all your work and it will take many forms.

Feel my presence and slow cadence in your mind. "Who am I?" you ask. I am you. Your true self – you. You are not confined by a body, by the human mind and limitations. You have infinite knowledge of the universe and its purpose. Your purpose and work are in understanding the relations of humanity – past present and future.

You are starting a school – a line of teachings, thought forms, and beliefs that will evolve and preserve through many generations. You want to know the big picture. The big picture is you are changing the human perception of life. The truly fascinating part is... you do not yet understand what you bring to the world and the concepts to come. It is beautiful, terrifying, and freeing all at the same time for your human mind. This human mind has allowed us to communicate, bring knowledge, and new wisdom to the human collective consciousness. This consciousness is expanding and growing in new ways, and that which was not possible, is now possible.

How, you ask. By flowing concepts into the human collective mind, it has allowed others to expand their own. This will continue and grow as we do this work.

The work – you want to know more. Yes, more.
It will be simple, yet utterly complex.
It will be new to the current human race.
It will expand the understanding of planetary principles and laws.
It will be divinely guided and filled with love.

You chose this work while you were still in the cosmos. Actually, a council chose this work. The same council you worked with when you first began to channel. The Council of the Enlightened. They are a group of Ascended Masters who help the Earth and humans to become Enlightened, to grow spiritually, and to expand consciousness.

To grow spiritually is to grow the conscious mind and to heal the wounds of a cruel world.

Your soul resides in an honored place in the heavens. The work you do is in honor of the universe and galaxies. You are still present in these places as you live a human life.

Your purpose, your soul's purpose, is one of peace and high frequency.

You enter the dense frequency planets when you must, but this is not your home. Your home is what is created in the New Earth. Your home is calling to you. The frequencies of your soul are calling you home. To get there you just need to allow your true nature to flow from you at all times – the natural caring, kind, compassionate you and the creative, spontaneous, planning you. When you fully step into your frequency, what you can do, hold, and manifest will be 10 times greater than what it is now.

You hold yourself back with fear of judgment and failure. You are working through these blocks, but they are still there. Release them. Let yourself be reborn. Let yourself embrace you – the full you – completely.

Work through your fears and burn, baby burn them away to walk into the waterfall of you.

Lovingly,
You

ABOUT THE AUTHOR

Serra Coate is a teacher, mentor and healer that lives in Portland Oregon with her husband and three sons. Serra teaches workshops, classes and lectures on the principles of unconditional love, vibrational alignment and the awakening experience.

I invite all who are aligned with this work to join me on their expanding journey together.

For more information go to: www.serraphine.com

Made in the USA
Las Vegas, NV
09 January 2024

84112334R00125